A Complete Survival Guide to Understand Empaths and Develop Empathy Abilities, Improve Your Emotional Intelligence, and Learn Strategies to Protect Yourself from Energy Vampires

— *JAKE NIGRAM* —

Legal Notice

© Copyright - All rights reserved.

No part of this book may be reproduced or transmitted in any form or any means, electronic or mechanical, including photocopying, recording, or by any information storage or retrieval system, without permission in writing from the Author and Publisher.

All the product names or logos described within this manual are the trademarks and/or copyrights of their respective owners.

The publication contains the opinions and ideas of its author and is designed to provide useful advice to the reader on the subject matter covered. Any references to any products or services do not constitute or imply an endorsement or recommendation.

The Author and Publisher strive to be as accurate and complete as possible in the creation of this book, but do not guarantee that the information or suggestion will affect everyone who reads it.

The Author and Publisher specifically disclaim any responsibility for any liability, losses or damages of any kind as a consequence, directly or indirectly arising from the use and/or application of any content of this publication.

Texts and images available over the Internet may be subject to copyright and other intellectual rights owned by third parties.

Disclaimer Notice

Please note the information contained within this document is for educational and entertainment purposes only.

Every attempt has been made to provide accurate, up to date and reliable complete information. No warranties of any kind are expressed or implied. Readers acknowledge that the author is not engaging in the rendering of legal, financial, medical or professional advice.

By reading this document, the reader agrees that under no circumstances are we responsible for any losses, direct or indirect, which are incurred as a result of the use of information contained within this document, including, but not limited to, errors, omissions, or inaccuracies.

TABLE OF CONTENTS

Empath
A Complete Survival Guide to Understand Empaths and Develop Empathy Abilities, Improve Your Emotional Intelligence, and Learn Strategies to Protect Yourself from Energy Vampires

INTRODUCTION..15

PART I: THE NATURE OF AN EMPATH........17

Chapter 1 Are You an Empath?.....................21

    Perspectives on empaths............................23

    Telling signs that you are an empath.........27

Chapter 2: The Different Types of Empaths that You Ought to Know 35

    Emotional empaths 37

    Spiritual (medium) empaths......................40

    Physiological empaths 41

    Geomantic (environmental) empaths 43

    Intuitive (cognitive/psychic/telepathic) empaths 45

Nature empaths (plant and animal) 46

Chapter 3: The SWOT of an Empath 50
Why SWOT? 50

Chapter 4: The Supernormal Powers of an Empath 60

The sensory power to detect, amplify, analyze and interpret faint signals 60

The compassionate power to serve 62

The intuitive power to gain an in-depth understanding of other people's emotions 63

The reflective power to counsel and mentor others to achieve their highest being 64

The fidelity power to be confidential and trustworthy 64

The solemn power to be alone, calm, and peaceful ... 65

PART II: MANAGING YOUR ENERGY AS AN EMPATH 67

Chapter 5: Why Managing Your Energy Matters 71

Chapter 6: Symptoms of Sapped Energy 73
How to tell if someone is draining your energy 75

Chapter 7: How to Protect Your Energy Reservoir as an Empath 77

Potential leakage points 78

Chapter 8: How to Recover and Rejuvenate Your Lost Energy 86

    Yoga 87
    Meditation 88
    Fitness workout 89
    Diet 89

Chapter 9: Recovering and Rejuvenating Your Mental Energy through Diet 91

    Key dietary principles to keep in mind 91
    Essential ingredients to remedy against stress, anxiety, and depression 93
    Dangers of bad sugar – Bad sugar contributes to many dangerous health conditions 104
    What kinds of food do I need to eat to boost Leptin reception? 107
    What kind of food must I keep off to avoid Leptin resistance? 108

Chapter 10: Recovering and Rejuvenating Your Mental Energy through Fitness Workouts 114

    The Benefits of Fitness exercise to Your Mental Health 114
    Why Exercises are Important for Stress Relief 122
    Simple Everyday Exercises that You Can Do to Relieve Stress 124
    Strategies to Help You Get Moving for Long 131

Chapter 11: Recovering and Rejuvenating Your Mental Energy through Mindfulness Meditation and Yoga 134

Mindfulness Meditation to rejuvenate your mental energy 135

- Yoga to Reinvigorate Your Energy Flow (Kundalini Yoga) 145
- Half Spinal Twist (Ardha Matsyendrasana) 147
- Spinal Flex (camel ride) 151
- Salabasana (Locust/Grasshopper Pose) 154
- Avasana (back-relaxation pose) 158
- Big Toe Pose (Padangusthasana) 163
- Bow Pose (Dhanurasana) 168
- Cat-Cow Pose (Marjaryasana-Bitilasana) 172
- Camel Pose (Ustrasana) 177
- Cobra Pose (Bhujangasana) 182
- Plow Pose (Halasana) 187
- Boat Pose (Naukasana) 192
- Fish Pose (Matsayasana) 196

PART III: MANAGING YOUR RELATIONSHIPS AND ENVIRONMENTS AS AN EMPATH 200

Chapter 12: How to Manage Your Work Environment and Boost Your Productivity as an Empath 203

Declutter 206

Keep time 209
- Work routine 209
- Evaluating day-to-day plan 210
- Rewarding success /Reprimanding failure 212

Avoid procrastination 216
- Know what to do 217
- Sharpen your resolve 218
- Device action plan...................................221
- Envision 222
- Dream 223
- Idealize 223
- Visualize 224
- Engender 224
- Assess...225
- SWOT your core inner variables 226
- Your mindset – the home to your inner variables ..228
- Carry out a Self SWOT Analysis....................228
- Strategize...228
- Creating a planning mindset.......................229
- Work on your mindset 230
- Why is mindset such important?...................230
- Vision: the place where your goal post ought to reside 231
- Why have a Vision?..................................231
- The three essential qualities of your vision 232

Work on your habit 240

Establish work boundaries 246

Chapter 13: How to Survive as an Empath 248

Keep boundaries 250

Keep off relationships that don't work 253

Detach yourself from the past 255

Detect energy vampires 257

How to handle energy vampires 265

How to deal with addiction 268

    Addiction triggers 269

    Emotions 270

    Phobia and anxiety 271

    Physical sensations 273

    Environmental triggers 274

    Places 274

    Things 275

    Situations 276

How to deal with codependency 278

    Parties to codependence 278

    How to break away from codependence 279

Master the power of NO! 282

Chapter 14: How to Raise an Empath Child
.... 284

How do you tell that your child is an empath? **285**

How to help an empath child deal with emotional issues **292**

How to help an empath child deal with relationship issues **298**

How to help an empath child deal with energy issues **299**

How to help an empath child achieve the highest level of creative aspirations **300**

PART IV: HOW TO MAINTAIN YOUR WELLBEING WHEN LIFE HURTS 301

Step One: Make a bold decision 304
So, what is a bold decision? 307
What is the first and foremost bold decision should you make? 310

Step Two: Take control of your situation . 313
What are the things that you cannot change? 316
What are the things that you can change? 317

Step Three: Take charge of your emotions 319
What is an emotion? 320
Why do you need emotions? 321
How do emotions come about? 324

Emotional intelligence 324
How to boost one's emotional intelligence 326
Willpower as the primary agent of self-regulation and control 327
What is willpower? 328
What breeds willpower? 330
The importance of emotional intelligence and willpower in healing a hurting life 331

Step Four: Be Focused 333

Change your mindset 337
What do you need in order to change your mindset? 339
Make your self-aware 340
Change your self-image 343
Regain your willpower: put your power and your will into action 344
Do start now! 346

Step Five: Engage the right association ... 348

Step Six: Give meaning to your life 357

Step Seven: Practice Self Compassion 365

CONCLUSION 380

INTRODUCTION

Empaths are some of the most misunderstood personality types. Being an empath means that you easily fall into this category of misunderstood personalities.

Yet, it is not just being misunderstood by the world, empaths misunderstand themselves when they do not cope with standards and expectations set up by a world dominated by non-empaths. Succumbing to conformity just to fit into the non-empaths' way of doing things is the most hurtful damage an empath can inflict on ownself.

This book, **Empath: A Complete Survival Guide to Understand Empaths and Develop Empathy Abilities, Improve Your Emotional Intelligence, and Learn Strategies to Protect Yourself from Energy Vampires**, is purposely written to clear these misunderstandings and enable empaths to avoid succumbing to conformity that maims their nature and mutes their voice.

Reading this guide, as an empath, you will learn ***how to discover yourself, improve your wellbeing and get the best out of your nature***.

Keep reading!

PART I: THE NATURE OF AN EMPATH

Overview

The entire life is a journey of discovery.

While it is easy to discover some aspects of our being, especially our performance against set standards, it is not easy to discover and identify ourselves in those aspects that are not standardized.

Yet, the bulk of our being is not standardized. There is no standard about our inherent nature of being. While standards may influence how you feel, and how you respond to certain things, they play a very minor role.

How you perceive things, how you react to external stimuli, how you create relationships, and how you control your emotions are all part of the inner mechanism – beyond that which standards can set, control and measure.

This inner mechanism, though entirely unique to you, can only be attributed to by certain observable traits that define your personality.

One such personality is EMPATH. An Empath is defined by a certain set of best-fitting personality attributes. They are best-fitting because no one empath is absolutely identical to another empath.

Even the so-called identical twins are not absolutely identical. Thus, there will be unique variations from one empath to another. However, their common traits make it easy to identify them, their needs, and their possible responses to a given set of external stimuli.

In this Part, we are going to explore the nature of an empath, different types of empaths, the supernormal powers of an empath, and ultimately, the SWOT (Strengths, Weaknesses, Opportunities, and Threats) of an empath.

The primary objective of this Part is to help you discover yourself... whether you are an empathy or not. And if you happen to be an empath, know that you are not alone.

What you may think is unique to you is shared by millions of others. With this knowledge, you will be able to discover yourself more and carry yourself with confidence.

In case you are not an empath, this Part will help you identify an empath near you... it could be your friend, your spouse, your child, your colleague, or any other significant person in your life... even a stranger you encounter for the first time.

Why is it such important to identify an empath around you? Empath responds differently to different kinds of communication.

Thus, being sensitive to their needs will not only help you avoid conflicting with them but also help you create a mutually beneficial relationship with them. In essence, you will become more empathetic about their nature of being.

Chapter 1
Are You an Empath?

Such a 'weird' question!

Yet, it is a very important question.

Many people go about their lives without realizing that they are empaths. Yet still, many assume that they are empaths while they are not. Answering this question helps to clear out this scenario.

Why ask?

This is a question that would most likely follow, albeit silently when some ask you "are you an empathy?" and it is deserved so. Why ask?

The reason why this question is fundamentally important is that; other factors remaining constant, the worldview and expectations of an empath are significantly different from that of a non-empath. Also, the reaction and response of an empath to a given situation will be characteristically different from that of a non-empath. And because of this, it is quite easy for an empath to be grossly misunderstood. This misunderstanding can bear a lot of burden on the empath, and worse of it, resulting in the empath's interests being injured.

Thus, answering this question helps to bring a deeper understanding, not only to oneself but also to those around you.

An empath is simply a person who exhibits a high level of sensitivity to the presence of other beings. This sensitivity is not only to other beings' emotions but also thoughts and posture.

Perspectives on empaths

While we have come up with a definition of who an empath is, it is highly generalized. This is deliberate. The main reason is that there are many different perspectives regarding the nature of an empath. The most prominent perspectives are psychological and spiritual.

A spiritual perspective on empaths

This is a perspective of the spiritualists' point of view.

Empaths are considered as people with a high level of spiritual power. Spiritually, empaths are considered as people with psychic ability to detect and interpret the other people's energy flows.

The most dominant of these energy flows is the emotional energy flow. Like professional they can sense this flow, dive in it, swim in it – the purpose and destiny vary depending on each circumstance. And like sailors, they can unfurl their sails to flow with this emotional current – again, the purpose and destiny vary depending on circumstances.

A psychological perspective on empaths

This is a perspective of the psychologists' point of view.

From a psychological perspective, an empath is considered to be a person with an extraordinary level of empathy – that is, the ability to read and interpret other people's emotional signals – and adjust their own state of being in response to these emotional signals.

The difference between spiritual and psychological perspectives

The fundamental difference between spiritual and psychological perspective is about **psychic power**.

Spiritual perspective regards empaths as people with psychic power. On the other hand, psychological perspective does not consider psychic power as what determines whether someone is an empath or not.

While psychological perspective does not object to the presence of psychic power, it does consider that someone can be empathetic without necessarily having psychic power.

It also considers that someone can also possess psychic power without necessarily being empathetic. Yes, we do have people with psychic power yet extremely narcissistic, which is extremely contrary to being empathetic.

Spiritual or psychological? Which way forward?

In this book, while we will not overlook the psychic attributes of an empath, we will bend heavily towards a psychological perspective.

Back to our primary question: Are you an empathy?

To answer this question, like all personality types, there is no clear boundary. However, certain predominant traits can prove a litmus test in detecting whether someone is an empath or not. These are the telling signs as to whether you are an empath or not.

Telling signs that you are an empath

The following are the key attributes of an empath:

1. *Supersensitive*

Empaths are highly sensitive. They can easily detect even the most passive of signals from those whom they are interacting with. They can easily gather sufficient cues to profile a person.

Due to their high sensitivity, they are emotionally turbulent as they flow with the waves emanating from different sources within their environment.

2. Superabsorbent

Empaths easily and quickly absorb other people's energy. This makes them emotionally attached and connected with people, especially those in need.

3. Super intuitive

This is the quality that makes many people to consider empaths as having psychic power. Empaths can easily predict situations. They can easily 'read' someone's mind. It is hard to lie to an empath.

Even though it is hard to lie to an empath, empaths easily fall into the deception trap... not because they haven't detected, but simply because they don't like turning people down. So, they may knowingly buy into a lie just because they don't want to hurt the feelings of the liar.

This super-intuitiveness is due to the strong emotional 'antenna' that powerfully scans and maps out a clear picture of the state of beings and state of things and thus be able to arrive at a clearer perspective.

4. Introverted

Though not all, most empaths are introverted. But, this does not necessarily mean that most introverts are empaths.

The best way to look at their introverted nature is from the perspective of whether they look inwards or outwards for solutions.

Introverts exhale their energy into others while extroverts inhale their energy from others.

As introverts, they feel uncomfortable with crowds, long chats, noisy environments, and such other clutters that sap off their energy.

5. Lone wolf

Empaths like spending time alone. They like enjoying their own space. They appreciate privacy than non-introverts do.

Being lone wolves is empaths' natural defense mechanism. It is a way to protect their energy levels and also recharge. Solitude is their recharge station.

6. Compassionate

Due to their intuitive and superabsorbent nature, most empaths are compassionate. They get moved by other people's difficult situations. They are deeply affected and have a high sense of guilt when they fail to help.

Being compassionate makes empaths magnetically attractive to children and animals. This is because both children and animals rely heavily on their intuition rather than logic.

Even adults find it easy to confide in an empath. Empathic persons become secret stores for other people because they are understanding, trustworthy, and bound to keep other people's secrets.

Another side of being compassionate is that empaths hate violence. They get deeply affected by cruelty towards others. Thus, they are natural peacemakers, mediators, and leaders. They are less aggressive, which is highly attractive to those who desire to be calmed.

The downside of being overly compassionate is that empaths end up getting very tired and fatigued – not just from taking care of others but overly thinking about others and thus draining their own mental and emotional energy.

7. *Nature-loving*

Introverts dissipate a lot of energy when they encounter other people, especially crowds. They also dissipate a lot of energy when they encounter unnatural vibrations and distractions. Thus, to be able to recharge and recover the dissipated energy, they get close to nature as possible. It is nature that recharges them. Getting close enables them to tap into natural energy reservoirs in vegetation, ground, water bodies, and even sky.

Taking a nature walk is what most empaths love. They love being close to plants and animals than being close to human beings. This is because plants and animals have a way of recharging them while other humans, especially non-empaths have a way of discharging them.

8. Easily overwhelmed by intimate relationships

Due to their susceptibility to being discharged by fellow human beings, empaths easily get overwhelmed by intimate relationships. Naturally, empaths love keeping distance. Keeping distance does not necessarily mean that they are cold-hearted.

On the contrary, empaths are deeply warm-hearted only that they lose a lot of this energy so quickly as a result of interacting with those who are relatively colder.

9. Highly reflective

Empaths have a very deep sense of reflection. This is because they detect many signals which enables them to have a clearer picture of the state of things than their non-empathetic counterparts.

10. Super-observant and extremely wise

Even though it may be argued that empaths are hardly street smart, this is more due to the compassionate nature that deters them from taking advantage of others and exploiting them.

They probably detect opportunities faster than their non-empathetic counterparts but are more reluctant to grab them. Their non-aggressive and non-competitive nature dissuades them from being first.

Furthermore, empaths are highly observant.

This makes them have a wait-and-see posture. They wait to see what non-empaths do when an opportunity presents itself and thus gain greater insight about the opportunity.

As a result, they gain greater wisdom. It is this greater wisdom that makes empaths highly dependable when it comes to giving advice.

Combined with their high sense of compassion, they become great advisors since they do not seek to take advantage of those seeking advice from them but rather feel compelled to genuinely help them. Furthermore, combined with their highly intuitive nature, they give advice that puts most probabilities into perspective.

The above are the 10 most significant attributes of empaths. If you possess at least 7 of them, then you are an empath.

Chapter 2: The Different Types of Empaths that You Ought to Know

In the previous chapter, we highlighted the common traits of empaths. Yet, some of the traits appeared nearly contradictory to others. Furthermore, it is hard to come across an empath who exhibits all those traits. Why?

The main reason is that not all empaths are the same. There are different types of empaths. This means that, although they do share certain traits in common, there are other traits that distinguish one type of empath from another.

While there are many different types of empaths, they are broadly classified into the following categories:

1. Emotional empaths

2. Spiritual empaths

3. Physiological empaths

4. Geomantic (environmental) empaths

5. Intuitive empaths

6. Nature empaths (plant and animal)

Emotional empaths

Emotional empaths are those who can easily pick up emotions of others and consequently synchronize their emotions to match those that they pick up.

This pushes emotional empaths to drown into the depth of other people's emotions.

Thus, an emotional empath will feel deeply sad when encountering a sad person, ecstatic when encountering an ecstatic person, and joyful when encountering a joyful person.

Emotional empaths lose their own emotions, or rather, their own emotions easily becomes obfuscated by the emotions of those around them. This makes emotional empathy experience chaotic emotions when in crowds because they can pull in all these different emotional signals and thus experience confusion and turmoil.

The challenge of being an emotional empath is the likelihood of suffering from psychosomatic illness – that is getting sick because of emotional stress. The pain of others becomes your pain – and their sickness can also become your sickness. You may not suffer the disease itself, but you simply suffer the pain and symptoms. As such, if tests are done, no disease is found yet you are suffering from the symptoms.

There are two types of emotional empaths:

- Affectionate empaths – they are superabsorbent when it comes to feelings of others. Thus, they become drenched and soaked with other people's feelings. They are emotional sponges.

- Compassionate empaths – the are drawn to act on the suffering of others. Other people's suffering is their Call-to-Action. A typical example of compassionate empaths is Mother Teresa.

Spiritual (medium) empaths

Spiritual empaths are those empaths who exhibit metaphysical capabilities. They can sense and communicate with supernormal realms. They have higher psychic abilities.

Spiritual empaths come as prophets, magic healers, foretellers, etc.

Spiritual empaths can detect non-physiological diseases and even heal them. They can provide remedies that bring healing to those suffering from nonphysiological illness.

While spiritual empaths played a prominent role in ancient traditions, they don't have a prominent role in modern times. This is not because they are less capable, but simply because of overreliance on science such that these abilities are neither encouraged nor promoted.

Physiological empaths

Physiological empaths are highly sensitive to the physical pain of others. Thus, they will do all they can to relieve other people's physical pain and suffering.

They suffer the pain of others and thus have to do something to relieve this suffering from themselves by dealing with that source of suffering... the pain of others.

Physiological empaths are easily drawn to the medical profession. Florence Nightingale is a typical example of physiological empaths. Nurses and doctors who choose their career out of calling rather than the pay package it offers are physiological empaths.

More often than not, physiological empaths are lost in the service of relieving other people's pain and thus end up feeling exhausted and burnout.

Because of their inability to control their feelings from being attached to the pain of others, they may end resentfully feeling drained. This makes it imperative for them to receive counseling, especially when encountering situations that cause pain on a massive scale such as disasters.

Physiological empaths are more susceptible to panic disorders, unexplainable pain, chronic depression, and chronic fatigue.

Geomantic (environmental) empaths

Geomantic empaths have a high level of sensitivity to the environment. Thus, they easily detect and interpret minute energy signals flowing from a given place. As such, they easily react to environmental changes.

This sensitivity can make geomantic empaths detect crime scenes, for example, a murder scene, and start feeling eerie. They may not tell exactly what took place at such a place but they will just feel extremely odd. Given little clues, they can easily cast a clearer image of what happened.

On the other hand, they can easily get excited about a place simply because something nice happened there – even without knowing exactly what happened there. For example, they can feel excited about visiting a place where there was a wedding party, a great picnic, etc.

When it comes to holy sites, they can easily become somber even when there is no sign indicating that such is a holy site.

Thus, geomatic empaths can make great detectives. They can also become great environmentalists and explorers.

Due to this sensitivity, the moods of geomantic empaths swings according to the place visited.

Intuitive (cognitive/psychic/telepathic) empaths

Intuitive empaths have a very deep sense of insight. They are highly reflective. They can easily collect very remote signals and connect them like jigsaw puzzles to come up with a clear picture of things.

Due to this ability, intuitive empaths can easily read people's thoughts by gathering signals from their eyesight, posture, behaviors, sweat scents, etc. They connect all these signals to cast the mental images flowing through the mind of a person.

Intuitive empaths possess precognitive powers. They can use the energy signals flowing to them to predict what kind of form these energy waves may collect into and thus come up with a clearer picture of that form.

Nature empaths (plant and animal)

Nature empaths have a high sensitivity to nature. Their energy flows highly synchronizes with the energy flow in nature.

Nature empaths can easily derive meaning from certain natural occurrences. For example, astrologists can derive meaning from the pattern of the stars, and even their appearances.

There are those nature empaths who can read from the wind flow and tell the potential likelihood of a dry season, observe the cloud patterns and tell the beckoning of rain season. Among very many others. Quite an amount of these has been backed up by the scientific establishment.

While nature empaths are in many different categories, the most prominent nature empaths are the flora (plant) empaths and fauna (animal) empaths.

Flora empaths

Flora empaths are highly intuitive about plant needs. They can tell when a plant needs water. They can tell when a plant is going to flower or not.

Flower empaths can tell when a plant is stressed or flourishing depending on the plant's posture and other signs.

Flora empaths gain a great depth of joy and happiness when plants flower, fruit, or just appearing healthy. They also derive great joy when they see a seed germinate. They would pinpoint to a particular seedling in the forest and devote their care to it.

Flora empaths can experience great agony, sorrow, and pain when they find out that a tree 'bleeds' or is 'wounded'. They become emotionally attached and feel as if the 'wound' and 'bleeding' is their own. They will feel irritated just as the sight or sound of an ax, sensing that it symbolizes harm or death to a tree.

Fauna empaths

Fauna empaths have a special affection and connection with animals. It becomes naturally easy for animals to befriend them. For example, wild animals feel comfortable being with a fauna empath when they would have ordinarily taken a flight or become aggressive in the presence of someone else.

Fauna empaths derive great joy and happiness when animals are playing, eating, or simply feeling good. This brightens their mood.

On the other hand, fauna empaths derive great pain and anguish when an animal dies, is brutally killed, is sick, injured or lack food. They will go to a greater extent trying to remedy the situation and won't be happy until the situation changes. Fauna empaths can greatly mourn and even get depressed by the death of an animal.

St. Francis of Assisi is a typical example of nature empath.

Chapter 3: The SWOT of an Empath

Empaths have their upside. But, like all other personality types, they do also have their downside.

It is important to consider the Strengths, Weaknesses, Opportunities, and Threats (SWOT) of this unique personality. Why?

Why SWOT?

The first and most important reason is to understand them. More often than not, empaths, being introverts, receive tons of criticism from non-empaths who get bewildered by their 'weird' nature. They are sometimes considered subnormal, especially when they are slow to act or react. Non-empaths expect them instantly swing into action and sometimes explode when faced with challenges. People don't understand that empaths take time to analyze what they perceive and decide the right cause of action against competition options.

The second reason is for them to take advantage of their strengths and opportunities available to them due to their unique nature. Due to the said criticism, many empaths never realize their strengths.

Most of their strengths are considered by many non-empaths as weaknesses. Thus, they are under constant pressure to mute their strengths. In identifying these strengths, they can gain an appreciation of them and thus stand by them.

There are plenty of opportunities available to empaths. We've seen them briefly in the previous chapter. In this chapter, we are going to expound on these opportunities.

Other than the empaths themselves, their friends and loved ones need to appreciate these strengths and beware of these opportunities so that they can take the supportive role of encouraging and inspiring the empaths.

The third reason is for them to take care of their weaknesses and guard against threats posed to them due to their unique nature. As we will see later, some of the perceived weaknesses of empaths can be their strengths. However, when empaths are unable to cover themselves from being taken advantage of, then, they cease to be strengths.

Threats to empaths are many. A high number of those people on the receiving end of codependence are empaths. Due to their empathetic nature, they are under constant threat of being taken advantage of by narcissists. Narcissists see them as preys.

Thus, knowing the threats that they encounter, they can be able to defend themselves. Also, with this knowledge, their friends and loved ones can take a proactive role to protect them, especially if they happen to be vulnerable minors.

Strengths of an empath

What are the strengths of an empath?

Empaths exhibit great strengths in uncharacteristic ways. The following are some of the great strengths of empaths:

- **They exhibit a relatively higher level of integrity** – since empaths like being of help to others and draw their strengths internally, they have a higher affinity towards integrity than non-empaths. Empaths like being truthful, both to themselves and others. They like being around genuine people and they easily get put-off by deceptive people.

- **They exhibit higher levels of compassionate altruism** – being lovers of truth; being more honest; and expecting the best of others, empaths rank higher on the scale of compassion and altruism compared to non-empaths. Compassionate altruism is the hallmark of most religious foundations. It is the foundation of most charity endeavors. It is the foundation of search for true freedom and liberty. Since empaths are greatly disturbed by the suffering of others, they are ready to pay the ultimate price to liberate others from pain and suffering. Thus, they take the role of being other people's saviors seriously.

- **They have a higher sense of alertness** – due to their high level of intuition, empaths can easily sense danger. If they practice relying on their intuition, then, they can easily save not only themselves but also others from harm.

- **They have a greater sense of neutrality** – empaths are less susceptible to biases due to their desire for truth. This, accompanied by their higher level of intuition, makes them more neutral as they cannot be easily swayed towards biases.

- **Reliable gut feelings** – everybody has gut feelings, but not everyone has reliable gut feelings. Empaths have more reliable gut feelings than non-empaths. This helps them deal with situations and make decisions where there are no established rules or procedures on how to detect and deal with such situations.

Weaknesses of an empath

- **Absorbing too much of other people's emotions** – empaths absorb too much of other people's emotions. They are other people's emotional sponges. As such, they easily get drenched by what goes around in other people's worlds. This makes them more susceptible to anxiety, stress, and depression. Non-empaths are not superabsorbent and thus can easily let other people's emotions drain off. Non-empaths are like umbrellas that don't allow much to enter through.

- **High tolerance for hurts** – while empaths easily detect situations, risks, and dangers, it doesn't necessarily mean that they easily escape harm. On the contrary, they are the most enduring and most persevering. The early detection, instead of helping them jump-off, it makes them harden their posture. They then endure up to the breakpoint. Thus, empaths are more susceptible to being persistently hurt.

- **More susceptible to burnout** – apart from absorbing too much emotional energy from others, empaths hardly tire from being involved in other people's suffering. Many of them overlook their own suffering just to alleviate other people's suffering. They have a high tolerance to burnout and thus can take in greater levels of fatigue. The end result is chronic burnout.

Opportunities available to an empath:

- **Positions of higher responsibility** – as we have indicated under strengths, empaths have a higher sense of integrity which draws them to become reliable, dependable and trustworthy. Thus, they are more likely to be looked out for to take positions of higher responsibility.

- **Championing causes for good** – due to their higher affinity towards compassionate altruism, empaths are often relied upon to take actions that help alleviate suffering by the vulnerable. They initiate and lead charity initiatives such as taking care of the destitute, refugees, disaster victims, victims of persecution, etc. They genuinely pursue justice for others.

- **Situational analysts** – due to their higher sense of alertness, empaths are best suited to handle on-the-ground situational analysis. This situational analysis could be about people's situations, environmental impact, among others.

- **Conflict management and resolution** – due to their greater sense of neutrality, accompanied by active listening ability, empaths are well suited to manage and resolve conflicts. Thus, they can serve as mediators, umpires, judges, diplomats, and such other positions that require one to balance various interests and bring about an amicable solution.

- **Intuitive decision-making** – since empaths have a more reliable gut feeling, they are more adept at making intuitive decisions. This makes them best suited to be advisors and mentors. Being an advisor and mentor relies heavily on intuition rather than written protocols.

Threats posed to an empath

- **Anxiety, stress, and depression** – due to them being other people's emotional sponges, empaths can easily get anxious, stressed, and depressed by other people's situations. Thus, empaths and their friends and loved ones should be conscious and heavily cautious about this threat. Most importantly, friends and loved ones should be ready to pull empaths out of emotionally demanding situations when they sense signs of fatigue, anxiety, and withdrawal.

- **Deep hurt and trauma** – do to their high tolerance for hurts, empaths can absorb a lot of injuries without backing off. This means that the wounds get deeper, healing process longer, and scars more permanent. To mitigate against this risk, empaths should be taught and put through practice mechanisms that lower their tolerance level towards common vulnerabilities such as codependency and narcissism.

- **Chronic burnout** – due to their high level of tolerance to fatigue, empaths often overwork themselves in solving other people's problems and alleviating their suffering to such an extent that they forget their own problems and suffering. This creates a multiplier effect in terms of the burdens that they are meant to carry. Since they hardly give up, they continue carrying thus the burden of fatigue and the end result is chronic burnout. Chronic burnout not only increases the mental risk of depression, but it also increases the risk of muscle burnout especially if they are carrying out physical chores in a bid to alleviate the suffering of others. Chronic burnout can cause severe health complications in the long-term thus reducing their opportunity to live healthily.

Chapter 4: The Supernormal Powers of an Empath

From the onset, we have persistently emphasized on the intuitive power of empaths. This is just one element of a whole set of supernormal powers that most empaths possess.

Let's consider some of these supernormal powers:

The sensory power to detect, amplify, analyze and interpret faint signals

Empaths are highly sensitive people. This makes them detect very faint energy signals that non-empaths cannot detect. They also expend a lot of energy towards amplifying these faint signals to meaningful levels.

They can detect these signals even in a noisy obfuscated environment such as where the signal generator tries to deliberately distort the signals. For example, when someone is trying to deceive to conceal the truth, trying to smile to disguise sorrow or anger, trying to show a serious face to mute laughter, etc. All these are obfuscating noises.

It is not easy to lie to empaths. And even if you succeed in a given moment, they will store the signals and start decoding them during the time they are quiet and alone. This is why they love solitude. It is at this moment that the amplification and decoding of faint obfuscated signals take place.

Due to this high sensory power, empaths are more likely than anyone else to possess psychic power. All they need is to practice active listening and not to ignore prompting signals. This is why most people with psychic power often spend a lot of time alone... and introverted empaths are great in this.

The compassionate power to serve

Empaths have the highest compassionate power than any other human being. This is because they can easily mark, step, and fit into other people's shoes.

In as far as problems are concerned, empaths are often other people's keepers. They are pain absorbers and the pain of others runs through them and thus makes them unable to be free from suffering unless they relieve the pain of others.

We know the importance of compassion in the world. It is compassion that serves refugees, seeks those buried under the rubble during earthquakes or bombs. They are the ones that build massive shelters for the displaced and equip free clinics and hospitals for those in need.

Empaths are the ones who quickly spring into action whenever a distress call rings. To an empathy, any distress about pain and suffering is, in essence, a Call-to-Action (CTA). They can never settle in peace until they answer the call.

The intuitive power to gain an in-depth understanding of other people's emotions

Knowing that most wars are due to conflicts. And that most conflicts are due to lack of in-depth understanding of other people's perceived threats, then it is easy to appreciate the importance of an in-depth understanding of other people's emotions.

It is this understanding of other people's emotions that enable empaths to be active listeners. It is also the same trait that makes them relatively calmer than non-empaths.

And this calm attitude makes them seek peace, and to be peacemakers. They are the most sought when conflicts arise. They are the most sought to give counsel, mediate and adjudicate intractable conflicts.

This is because they can dig deeper into the emotional state of the parties to a conflict and get what each party is not presenting on the table... either deliberately or for lack of better ways to bring it up.

The reflective power to counsel and mentor others to achieve their highest being

By virtue of an in-depth understanding, empaths can have a bigger and clearer picture of other people's intents. They can also easily map out their path and visualize their destiny. This way, they can easily counsel against bad intents, be it deliberate or not.

On the other hand, they can mentor others on the best way to achieve their good intents. This is because, like a torchbearer in the dark, they can 'see' what others are not seeing and thus be able to warn them against pitfalls, risks, and dangers that they ought to be cautious about in their journey.

The fidelity power to be confidential and trustworthy

Since most empaths are introverts, they do not easily reveal their thoughts. They do not struggle to keep secrets. Keeping secrets comes as a natural occurrence to them rather than a forced circumstance.

Combined with being active, compassionate, and empathetic listeners, they easily attract those who seek trust and confidentiality.

Thus, it is common to find empathetic persons being given sensitive positions of responsibility that requires utmost good faith, extreme confidentiality, and strong trust such as umpires, pastors, arbitrators, mediators, diplomats, envoys, etc.

The solemn power to be alone, calm, and peaceful

Empaths are sometimes considered abnormal due to their ability to comfortably stay quiet and enjoy solitude. Most extroverts (who are mostly non-empaths) easily get scared by solitude and get disturbed by silence.

Yet, the power to be alone, calm, and peaceful is extremely important. It enables one to declutter the mind, find meaning out of chaos, have a deeper insight, and reflect greatly on happenings.

This means that empaths can think in ways that most non-empaths cannot. Hence, they can come up with solutions to situations that would have hardly come by if there were no empaths.

PART II: MANAGING YOUR ENERGY AS AN EMPATH

Overview

We are all energy entities. Life is nothing but a bundle of vibrating energy.

We gain and dissipate energy. There are those things that enable us to become energized. Yet, others make us lose energy.

How we gain and dissipate energy is greatly influenced by our personality type. Things that make empaths lose energy may cause non-empaths to gain energy. On the other hand, certain things that make non-empaths lose energy make empaths gain energy.

Since empaths are not in the majority, it means that they are more susceptible to losing energy. This is because, just like other humans, they are social beings. They are bound to interact with other social beings.

Naturally, in social interactions, almost all beings seek to interact in such a way that they gain energy.

However, since empaths are more likely going to lose energy in situations where non-empaths are more likely to gain it, it follows that empaths have to cautiously guard their energy in such kinds of interactions.

Every reaction has an impact on the energy level. There are those reactions that bring in more energy while there are those others that dissipate more energy.

What is important is for empaths to know those reactions that can cause them to lose more energy. Thus, they can either avoid situations that are likely going to trigger such reactions or simply try to be in control of such reactions so that they do not overreact.

In this Part, we are going explore different ways by which empaths can manage their energy in such a manner that does not endanger their health and overall wellbeing. We begin by looking as to why managing energy matters so much to an empath.

We go further to explore how an empath can protect own energy reservoir so that it does not get extravagantly depleted to dangerous levels.

The depleted energy level is dangerous to the health and wellbeing of an empath. This is why it is important for an empath to quick identify depleted energy levels and take appropriate remedial action.

While most empaths can easily sense symptoms of depleted energy, very few know that these symptoms are actually about energy depletion and not anything else. Thus, it is important to identify these symptoms and what each means in terms of energy depletion.

After identifying energy depletion, the next important thing to do is to replenish and restore the lost energy.

In this Part, we are going to explore ways by which an empath can recharge, replenish lost energy stock, and rejuvenate to higher energy levels.

Chapter 5: Why Managing Your Energy Matters

Every signal is an energy signal.

We've seen that empaths dissipate a lot of energy. This energy dissipates in the cause of processing different kinds of signals.

While everyone is a signal generator and signal receiver, empaths are more of signal receivers than signal generators.

As we have indicated, most empaths are introverted. Thus, they listen a lot and say a little. This is as opposed to extroverts who say a lot and listen a little.

Signal receiver incurs a lot of energy to scan, detect, receive, convert and interpret signals. This is unlike the signal generator whose main task is to generate and transmit signals. Thus, given the same signal, the signal receiver will spend a lot more energy on it than the generator that created and transmitted the said signal. This is why introverts find themselves losing a lot of energy in social interactions while extroverts tend to gain a lot from it.

This means that empaths are more likely to suffer from energy deficit, hence the need to manage their energy more closely.

The consequences of energy deficit are dire. Physically, this can bring fatigue and even pain. Mentally, this can bring anxiety, stress, and depression. Psychologically, this can trigger suicidal tendencies.

Chapter 6: Symptoms of Sapped Energy

To effectively manage your energy reservoir, it is important to know when it is getting low. Symptoms are the best indicators.

The following are the common telling signs that your energy is getting sapped out:

- **Hopelessness** – when your mental and emotional energy goes down, you start feeling hopeless. Hopelessness means that you are unable to fuel positive thoughts which require more vibrancy than negative thoughts.

- **Sudden irritability** – when, all of a sudden you start feeling irritable without being able to tell why, then, that simply means that your mental and emotional energy is draining out sharply.

- **Insomnia** – insomnia has many causes. Being drained of energy can be one of the causes. Loss of physical energy can easily drive you to sleep, but not loss of mental and emotional energy that makes you remain agitated when you ought to relax. Signals about the loss of mental and emotional energy are similar to hunger signals. They may cause you a loss of sleep.

- **Loss of motivation** – motivation is simply an outcome of an excited mental and emotional energy. When your energy levels are low, there is a lack of excitation and thus loss of motivation.

- **Detachment** – detachment is a natural self-defense mechanism that seeks to remove you from that person, being, object, or sensation that is draining your energy. Detachment can be expressed in the form of not wanting to interact with people you often love interacting with, not wanting to engage in activities that you often like engaging in, etc.

- **Physical distress** – extreme situations of sapped energy such as stress and depression can cause physical distress. This physical distress can be expressed in terms of aching, painful joints, stomach problems, etc.

- **Chronic fatigue** – inability to replenish lost energy for a long time or persistent drain that results in chronic depletion results in chronic fatigue. With chronic fatigue, you become lethargic and thus no longer feeling energetic enough to carry out tasks or participate in activities that were hitherto easy to do.

How to tell if someone is draining your energy

Energy vampires are the worst energy drainers. Thus, it is important to know when you are in the presence of an energy vampire so that you can be able to keep off.

The following are telling signs that you are in the presence of an energy vampire:

- You think about them all the time – in a negative way
- You get physically exhausted while in their presence
- You feel relieved when they leave
- You feel pushed too much by their demands
- You feel more frustrated in your conversation with them than you were before
- You feel like withholding a lot from them
- You feel that you want to be alone for a while after they leave
- You feel demoralized and loss of motivation in their presence

Chapter 7: How to Protect Your Energy Reservoir as an Empath

Empaths are more susceptible to expending more energy than they are receiving. Thus, it is common for empaths to have an energy deficit.

The negative consequences of severe energy deficit make it imperative for empaths to device ways and means to protect their energy reservoirs from getting dangerously low.

To be able to protect your energy reservoir from leaks, you need to know potential leakage points.

Potential leakage points

As we have indicated, empaths are likely to suffer from the chronic energy deficit. This is due to the higher likelihood of more outflow than inflow.

The following are potential leakage points:

- Crowds
- Pollution
- Clutter
- Humanitarian crisis
- Eerie spaces
- Energy vampires

Crowds

Empaths are generally signal recipients. Thus, they probe, receive, synthesize and respond to signals from others. Like any other signal receiver, signals from multiple sources result in higher energy consumption, confusion and at times some signals obfuscate others. This makes the signal receivers to be overwhelmed and even break down.

The same is the case with empaths. Empaths like one-on-one encounters. They are great at dialogue. They are active listeners. Active listening requires higher energy concentration. When different sources compete for the active listener, the energy gets overdrawn. This is why empaths become more anxious, irritated, and stressed by the mere presence of crowds.

Thus, it is natural for empaths to avoid crowds and crowded places. However, sometimes situations, especially certain kinds of jobs, forces them to be in crowds or work with crowds.

How to protect oneself from being drained by crowds

- **Get yourself distracted** – you can get yourself distracted from the crowds. You can achieve this by putting on an earphone. You can also pick one person whom you decide to engage in a deep one-on-one conversation and that puts all your attention away from the crowd and to the conversation.

- **Make yourself busy** – one of the ways to avoid getting too much absorbed by the sensitivity to the crowds is to get yourself busy. Being physically busy will obviously drain your physical energy but not as much as mental and emotional energy that you would lose when you focus on listening to the crowds. Seek an opportunity to serve the crowd. For example, you can choose to be an usher, a waiter, or even an errand person.

- **Avoid unnecessary crowds** – be selective about the social events you attend. Those that are not important, turn down the invitation or delegate if possible.

- **Make your attendance as brief as possible** – If you happen to attend, find ways to excuse yourself so that you do not spend a lot of time with the crowd to such a level that you feel bored and irritated. Endeavor to leave the crowd while you still feel good. Don't stay to that point that you no longer feel happy. Leave at the climax of things.

Environmental Pollution

Noise pollution, water, and air pollution are the two common irritants to empathetic persons. They easily push an empathetic person into thinking so much about them. For example, an empathetic person will be so concerned about the welfare of children in such an environment, the welfare of the sick, different kinds of risks, etc. Even bad memories about the effect of such pollution can be triggered and thus drain the empaths mental energy.

The empath will be thinking about what to do about it. And if the empath feels incapable of doing anything he/she will feel stressed, discouraged, and overwhelmed.

Clutter

Most empaths are highly sensitive to clutter. The presence of a cluttered space disorients them. This is because the clutter sucks energy from them. They end feeling exhausted. To react to this exhaustion, most empaths become irritable, moody, stressed and more aggressive.

The following are some of the clutters that can have a profound negative effect on the empaths:

- Trash clutter
- Color clutter
- Motion clutter
- Scent clutter
- Mind clutter

How to protect oneself from being drained by clutter:

- Tidy and organize your space – be it the bedroom, living room, study room, or office.

- if possible, keep off cluttered public space that you have no means of tidying or rallying people to do so.

- In case you are in an untidy place where you may not have the power to tidy – for example, when you are someone's guest, try to draw your attention away from the clutter until you leave. You can excuse yourself to leave or if inappropriate, find ways to take a walk away from the clutter. For example, if it is the living room that is cluttered, you may draw your attention towards a flower outdoor and request your host to explore it.

Humanitarian crisis

Most empaths are driven into action mode whenever a humanitarian crisis happens. Unlike non-empaths, most empaths are deeply involved. They go beyond physical and invest a lot of their emotions and thinking into a given crisis. Even after leaving the crisis scene, they can't switch off their minds and emotional attachment to the scene.

This makes empaths feel extremely drained.

Eerie spaces

Eerie spaces are those spaces that make you uncomfortable due to the negative energy that is contained in them. They could be a crime scene, ruins of war, shrines for satanic rituals, among others. Such places are like a giant suction pump.

If you are a psychic empath, then, such places will drain your energy since you will be exposed to psychic forces eager to suck off your energy.

Energy vampires

Energy vampires are those people who, when you encounter them or interact with them, you end up losing a lot of your energy to them.

Energy vampires have a way of sucking off your mental and emotional energy through devious means of dark psychology. It may be deliberate or even unknown to them that they are sucking off your energy.

Whenever you detect energy vampires, keep off them.

Chapter 8: How to Recover and Rejuvenate Your Lost Energy

As an empath, losing your mental and emotional energy is quite easy. You are more susceptible to this loss of energy than non-empaths.

The biggest risk of losing this energy is that you can easily suffer from stress and anxiety. And if this energy loss remains chronic, you may snap into depression. Thus, stress, anxiety, and depression are some of the most common risks facing empaths.

To make sure that you guard yourself against these risks, then, you must find ways to quickly recover and rejuvenate your lost energy.

Unlike non-empaths who can recharge their lost energy through social interactions, empaths hardly find suitable candidates to recharge. Thus, they run a higher risk of discharging rather than recharging through social interactions. This is why when they feel drained they opt for solitude.

The following are the best ways by which empaths can recharge their lost energy:

- Yoga
- Meditation
- Fitness workouts/exercises
- Proper diet (especially mental diet)

Yoga

Yoga is a set of ancient fitness exercises that are aimed at streamlining energy flows. They are slow, gradual, and reflective posture-based exercises.

The primary focus is to release clogged energy paths. When energy paths are clogged, it means that energy is not flowing well and thus it is not properly distributed throughout the body. The consequence is that some body organs are inadequately supplied with this energy. The most started body part is the brain since it takes a lot of effort for energy to be pumped up to the head.

For more information on how to recover and rejuvenate your lost energy through yoga, please read Chapter 11.

Meditation

Like Yoga, meditation is one of the ancient ways of recovering and rejuvenating your mental energy.

A lot of times, yoga and meditation are blended together to optimize energy recovery and rejuvenation.

For more information on how to use meditation to recover and rejuvenate your lost energy, please read Chapter 11.

Fitness workout

One of the easiest ways to boost your lost mental and emotional energy is to carry out fitness exercises. Fitness workouts are quite fast in this regard. However, in case you find your mental energy still getting chronically depleted even with fitness workout, then, it is important to combine your fitness workout with other remedies such as meditation and diet.

For more information on how to use fitness exercises to recover and rejuvenate your lost energy, please read Chapter 10

Diet

More often than not, empaths are more susceptible to stress, anxiety, and depression when frequently exposed to conditions that persistently lower their energy levels. They are also bound to experience a lot of mental fatigue.

Thus, empaths suffer more from mental exhaustion than physical exhaustion. To be able to protect mental energy reserves and replenish depleted stock, empaths need to take a diet that helps to replenish their mental energy.

For more information on how you can use diet to recover and rejuvenate your lost mental energy, please read Chapter 9

Chapter 9: Recovering and Rejuvenating Your Mental Energy through Diet

Not all foods are the same when it comes to mental energy and health. Some foods are mental energy stressors while others are mental energy rejuvenators.

Key dietary principles to keep in mind

- Eat a balanced diet rich in nutrients

- Take plenty of water

- Practice clean eating – that is, eat foods as close to their natural form as possible

- Grace your plate with essential anti-oxidants

- Avoid bad sugar
- Eat protein-rich foods to boost alertness
- Eat a Mediterranean-type diet
- Get enough vitamin D
- Eat selenium-rich foods
- Include Omega-3 fatty acids

Mental energy rejuvenators

These are foods that promote the fight against stress and depression. They include;

- Water – clean, natural drinking water.
- Vegetables, especially dark green leafy vegetables.
- Fruits, especially those rich in Vitamin C.
- Oil-rich fish, especially that rich in Omega-3 fatty acids.
- Whole grains.

Mental energy stressors

These are foods that trigger or aggravate stress and depression. They include;

- Bad sugar
- Caffeine
- Alcohol
- Gluten-rich foods (especially those who are allergic to gluten)
- Dairy milk products (except cheese, plain yogurt, and naturally sour/fermented milk)
- Saturated fat

Essential ingredients to remedy against stress, anxiety, and depression

The following are essential ingredients to consider in your diet and their respective remedies;

- **Omega-3 fatty acids** - depression and loss of memory
- **Dietary fiber** - depression
- **Folic acid** – depression, anxiety
- **Selenium** – depression, and irritability
- **Zinc** – depression, confusion, blank mind, lack of motivation and loss of appetite
- **Tyrosine** – depression, lack of motivation
- **Tryptophan** – depression
- **Magnesium** – depression, insomnia, stress, irritability, and anxiety
- **Vitamin B1** – depression, poor concentration and lack of attention
- **Vitamin B3** – depression
- **Vitamin B5** – depression and memory loss
- **Vitamin B6** – depression, irritability, stress and memory loss

- **Vitamin B12** – depression, confusion, memory loss
- **Vitamin C** - Depression

Superfoods to consider

The following are foods rich in ingredients necessary to prevent and stop stress, anxiety, and depression;

- **Foods rich in omega-3 fatty acids** – oily sea fish e.g. (salmon, herring, mackerel, sardines, pilchards, fresh tuna, trout), walnuts, flaxseeds, etc.
- **Foods rich in fiber** – green leafy vegetables, complex carbohydrates, whole grains, etc
- **Foods rich in folic acid** –vegetables (spinach, asparagus, lettuce, broccoli, Brussels sprouts, fresh parsley, savoy cabbage, beetroot, green peas, cauliflower) , meat (calf liver, turkey), oily sea fish (cod, tuna, salmon, halibut, shrimp) , nuts and seeds (hazelnuts, peanuts, walnuts, sesame seeds, cashew nuts),

beans and pulses (kidney beans, black beans, chickpeas, pinto beans, lentils), fruits (oranges, avocados).

- **Foods rich in selenium** – vegetables (garlic, mushroom, spinach), fish (cod, tuna, halibut, salmon, shrimp), whole grains (wheat germ, brewers' yeast, barley, oats, long-grain brown rice), beans and pulses (tofu), meat (calf liver, turkey breast), nuts (brazil nuts), dairy (mozzarella cheese), seeds (sunflower, mustard)

- **Foods rich in zinc** – meat (turkey, chicken (dark meat), lamb, beef, pork), vegetables (mushrooms, spinach, broccoli, asparagus, squash), fruit (kiwi, blackberry), nuts (almonds, walnuts, cashew nuts), seafood (shrimp, oysters, mussels), whole grain cereals, beans and pulses (miso, lima beans, baked beans, kidney beans, chickpeas), dairy (cheese and plain yoghurt), seeds (sesame, pumpkins), whole roasted sweet potatoes (especially the skin).

- **Foods rich in Tyrosine** – vegetables (spinach, green beans, soy sauce, miso soup, tofu), sour dairy products (cheese, plain yoghurt), lean meat (turkey, beef liver, chicken liver, tuna), fruits (avocados, tomatoes, bananas, prunes, figs, plums, raisins)

- **Foods rich in Tryptophan** – vegetables (cabbage, spinach, watercress), beans and pulses (soya beans, lima beans, kidney beans, lentils, chickpeas), lean meat (skinless chicken and skinless turkey), sour dairy products (cheese and plain yoghurt), eggs, nuts (hazelnuts, pistachios peanuts, almonds, soy nuts), seeds (sesame seeds, pumpkin seeds, poppy)

- **Foods rich in Magnesium** – fruits (kiwi, avocado, berries, banana, oranges, raisins), vegetables (spinach, Brussels sprouts, pepper, watercress, broccoli, green cabbage), nuts (almonds, cashew nuts, peanuts, walnuts, pistachios ,brazil nuts, macadamia), seeds (sesame seeds, sunflower seeds, pumpkin seeds, poppy), whole grains (quinoa, oatmeal, barley, buckwheat, bran, long-grain rice), dairy (plain yoghurt), beans and pulses (baked beans).

- **Foods rich in Vitamin B1** – vegetables (spinach, mushrooms, broccoli, asparagus, cabbage, Brussels sprouts, watercress, aubergine, lettuce, peppers, green peas), beans and pulses (soya milk, lentils), meat (pork), nuts (pine nuts, pistachios ,brazil nuts, hazelnuts), seeds (sesame seeds, sunflower seeds), fish and seafood (mussels, tuna, salmon), whole grain (oats, barley, fresh pasta, brown rice)

- **Foods rich in Vitamin B3** – vegetables(broccoli, Brussels sprouts, mushrooms, squash, courgette), nuts (peanuts), meat (turkey, chicken, pork, beef liver and kidney), fish (salmon, tuna), whole grains (wheat germ, brown rice, rice bran), seeds (sunflower)

- **Foods rich in Vitamin B5** – vegetables (broccoli, mushrooms, sweet potatoes, watercress, cauliflower, celery, carrots, peas, alfalfa sprouts), fruits (lemon, strawberries, raspberries, blackberries, watermelons), beans and pulses (chickpeas, broad beans), fermented dairy (yoghurt), whole grains (oats, wheat germ, brown bread, bran)

- **Foods rich in Vitamin B6** – vegetables (potatoes, asparagus, cauliflower, cabbage, bok choy, watercress, peppers, squash), fruits (avocados, mangoes, bananas), beans and pulses (chickpeas, soybeans, lima beans), whole grains (oats, barley, brown rice, bran), fish (tuna, salmon, trout), meat (turkey, chicken, pork loin), seeds (sunflower)

- **Foods rich in Vitamin B12** – fish and seafood (tuna, salmon, halibut, bass, oyster, shrimp, clams, crab), meat(turkey, chicken, lamb, calf liver), dairy (cottage cheese, low-fat yogurt, dairy or poached eggs, milk),

- **Foods rich in Vitamin C** – fresh fruits (oranges, tangerines, pineapples, strawberries, cranberries, papaya, kiwi, cantaloupe), vegetables (brussels sprout, red pepper, broccoli, cauliflower, red cabbage, kales, celery, watercress, squash)

Types of diet to consider

- Gluten-free diet
- Sugar-free diet
- CRAP-free diet
- Caffeine-free diet
- Leptin boosting diet
- Vegetarian diet
- Herbal diet
- Mediterranean diet
- Dietary herbs – green and red pepper, rosemary, garlic, sage, among others.

Gluten-free Diet

Gluten is one of the most controversial diets in as far as depression is concerned. There are those experts who advise against it while others do not. Nonetheless, there is concurrence that gluten is dangerous to those who suffer from celiac disease or are generally allergic to gluten. Limited scientific studies have found some correlation between gluten and depression but haven't conclusively established how gluten contributes to depression.

The general advice would be to limit the intake of gluten if you are experiencing symptoms of depression. If you are suffering from celiac disease, then, the gluten-free policy should be your inevitable choice. However, if you are not suffering from celiac disease or you are not in any way allergic to gluten, then, you mustn't consider avoiding gluten foods since these foods are rich in other essential nutrients that your body needs.

Foods rich in gluten include wheat and wheat products such as bread, pasta, cakes, among others. Also, barley and rye are rich in gluten.

Sugar-free Diet

Like gluten, sugar is another controversial component of our diet. Some advocate for the total ban of sugar and declaration of it as a dangerous product. Yet, some advocate for it to be taken but in moderation while others don't see anything wrong with it.

However, not all sugar is bad. What is bad is simple sugar but not complex sugar.

Many studies have established a correlation between bad sugar and depression. Thus, to avoid depression or mitigate its symptoms, you ought to avoid bad sugar.

Good sugars vs Bad sugars

Besides the simple sugars and complex sugars, we can also categorize sugars as good sugars or bad sugars.

As a rule of thumb, simple sugars are generally bad sugars while complex sugars are generally good sugars. This is because simple sugars are rapidly absorbed into the bloodstream thus easily causing spikes that destabilize the blood sugar level. Complex sugars take time to digest and therefore are gradually absorbed into the bloodstream which hardly destabilizes sugar levels.

However, naturally occurring glucose and fructose, if consumed in natural form are not dangerous to your health. Glucose is the primary source of energy for your body. What is bad is processed glucose and processed fructose and which must be avoided at all costs.

Simple sugars

Simple sugars are simple carbohydrates that get easily digested and utilized by the body. Simple sugars include glucose, fructose, lactose, sucrose, maltose, and monosaccharides.

Complex sugars include

Complex sugars are complex carbohydrates that take time to be digested and utilized by the body. Examples of complex carbohydrates include cellulose, dextrin, glycogen, and starch. These complex carbohydrates are commonly found in vegetables, wholemeal bread, and cereals. Foods rich in complex carbohydrates include spinach, whole grains, broccoli, yams, beans, lentils, skimmed milk, zucchini, and most leguminous plants.

Dangers of bad sugar – Bad sugar contributes to many dangerous health conditions

Apart from depression, bad sugar is responsible for triggering or aggravating the following diseases (which, in one way or another, also contributes to depression);

- Obesity
- Type II diabetes
- Hypertension
- Gastric or duodenal ulcers
- Various forms of allergies

- Dementia
- Cell death
- Kidney disease
- Premature aging
- Cataracts
- Liver disease
- Gout
- Over 100 other illnesses

CRAP-free Diet

CRAP (Carbonated, Refined, Alcoholic/Artificial additives and Processed) foods are dangerous to your health. This is one area where most health experts concur. Studies have found out that CRAP foods negatively affect neurotransmitters thus causing depression.

Some of the CRAP foods to avoid include;

- Carbonated products such as sodas

- Refined products such as table sugar and table salt,

- Alcoholic products such as those that contain concentrated levels of alcohol exceeding 40% Vol. such as spirit and certain kinds of beer. Artificial additives such as artificial sweeteners (including sucralose {Splenda}, Acesulfame Potassium, Aspartame, Neotame, and Saccharine) have been known to compromise neurotransmitters responsible for guarding against depression.

- Processed foods. Processed foods are usually devoid of essential nutrients and rich fiber. It is important to practice clean eating, that is, eating foods as close to their natural form as possible.

Leptin Diet

Leptin is a hormone secreted by adipose (fatty) tissue. It is responsible for the control of hunger and the feeling of satiety.

Certain foods help to trigger and boost Leptin secretion thus bringing the feeling of satiety for long. Once you feel satisfied for long, your cravings and hunger for food are kept at bay. Thus, the extra carbohydrates that are required to be stored into the body as excess fat are avoided altogether. The net result is that you lose unnecessary weight while gaining on lean muscles as most of such foods are known to build stronger muscles.

Studies have found out that Leptin resistance is primarily responsible for obesity. Obesity is one of the leading causes of depression. Thus taking a leptin receptive diet will help you keep off obesity and overweight which in the end will help you prevent or remedy depression.

What kinds of food do I need to eat to boost Leptin reception?

The following are categories of foods that you need to take to boost your Leptin reception;

- Complex carbohydrates

- Protein foods (especially plant sources of protein fiber and sea sources of protein)

- Low glycemic vitamin sources (such as vegetables and low-sugar fruits)

What kind of food must I keep off to avoid Leptin resistance?

As a rule of thumb, the following are categories of foods that you must avoid to keep off Leptin resistance;

- Simple carbohydrates

- Bad sugars

- CRAP (Carbonated, Refined, Alcoholic/Artificial Additives and Processed) foods.

Vegetarian Diet

A vegetarian diet has been known to contain a good amount of elements necessary for the proper functioning of neurotransmitters responsible for fighting depression. However, unless due to unavoidable circumstances that restrict you to a vegetarian diet, it is prudent to include animal sources of essential nutrients that fight depression.

Herbal Diet

Herbs have been known for long to aid in fighting depression. Prominent among them include St. John's Wort, Valerian and Passionflower. Apart from these, there are certain herbs, though not directly responsible for fighting depression are essential as catalysts and substitutes to harmful ingredients. These include;

- **Sugar substitutes** - Stevia is a plant that has sugar that is several times sweeter than table sugar yet has no calories. It is great for those who desire to lose weight as it adds no calories.

- **Salt substitutes** (not pure substitutes but offers an alternative taste to the plain food) – parsley, thyme, oregano, bay, sage, mint, chives, tarragon, fennel, savory, rosemary, among others. These can enable you to prevent intake of excess salt thus avoiding a counterbalancing demand for sugar to neutralize it.

- **Ginger** – ginger has been known to help in digestion and boosting food absorption. This acts as a catalyst for the intake of essential ingredients in the prevention and fights against depression.

- **Pepper** – pepper has been known to be a rich source of Vitamin C and plenty of other essential ingredients that aid in fighting depression.

To help prevent depression, you need to:

- **Eat plenty of vegetables and fruits**: It is recommended that men should eat 3 cups of vegetables per day and 2 ½ cups of fruits per day. It is also recommended that women should eat 2 ½ cups of vegetables and 1½ cups of fruits per day.

- **Take a diet rich in potassium.** Fruits and vegetables provide much-needed potassium. Potassium is important in maintaining healthy blood pressure levels. Deficiency in potassium can result in high blood pressure. High blood pressure can damage the linings of arteries inside your brain thus making them hard and brittle which can make them break or block blood flow. Important sources of potassium include tomatoes, spinach, bananas, apricots, broccoli, avocado, unpeeled potatoes (both Irish and Sweet potatoes), oranges, prunes and legumes (especially white beans and lima beans)

- **Eat stroke-preventing fruits**. Apples, Pears and white fruits and vegetables have been found to minimize the chances of onset of stroke.

- **Eat fruits that slow down cognitive aging**. Berries have been found out to slow down cognitive aging. Berries, especially blueberries and strawberries are rich in anthocyanins, which are known to slow down cognitive aging.

- **Eat fish rich in Omega-3 fatty acids (DHA-rich fish)**. A study has found out that older adults who ate fish at least once or twice a week had a greater volume of grey matter in areas responsible for Alzheimer's disease and thus resulted in a slower rate of developing dementia or cognitive impairment. The study further found out that only 3.2% of those who ate fish once or twice a week developed either dementia or cognitive impairment compared to 31% of those who don't consume fish. The main component in fish responsible for this is Omega-3 fatty acid, DHA. Another study established that DHA plus lutein increased verbal fluency, caused improvement in memory and learning. Taking more of DHA-containing fish increases DHA in the brain's grey matter.

- **Eat healthy fats.** A study published in 2012 found out that older women who ate the most saturated fat had poor scores on both cognitive function and memory tests compared to those who ate mono-saturated fats who exhibited high cognitive and memory functions. Foods rich in mono-saturated fats include olive oils, canola oils, and nuts.

- **Take tea.** Tea has been known to contain the highly neuroprotective amino acid L-theanine. This amino acid has both antioxidant and anti-inflammatory mechanisms and other properties that cause a reduction in brain levels of amyloid-beta. Amyloid-beta is an abnormal protein that is known to be a factor contributing to Alzheimer's disease.

Chapter 10: Recovering and Rejuvenating Your Mental Energy through Fitness Workouts

It is a known fact that fitness workouts greatly boost your mental energy. Nonetheless, we can have special attention to this mental energy booster for empaths.

The Benefits of Fitness exercise to Your Mental Health

Fitness exercise is one of the commonest physical activities engaged by humankind since time immemorial as a way of survival and meeting daily needs. Unfortunately, with the advent of modernity characterized by conveniences of cars, motorbikes, airplanes, railway lines, lifts, escalators, among others and with the increasingly expanding work and study schedules, time and incentives for fitness exercise have actively diminished. This has led to a sedentary lifestyle to set in.

It cannot be over-emphasized that the sedentary lifestyle kills. Most of the poor health conditions that we currently experience are due to lack of physical activity, more so, fitness exercise. Obesity, heart disease, cardiovascular disease, diabetes, mental disorders, some forms of cancers, among many other unhealthy conditions are either directly or indirectly attributed to a sedentary lifestyle.

The benefits of fitness exercise to your mental health are many and immense. The following are 15 key benefits of fitness exercise to your mental health;

1. **Fitness exercise helps to prevent and relieve anxiety** – anxiety arises out of being over-conscious about something imminent. When doing a fitness workout, the focus shifts away from that imminent concern to your fitness exercise. In this

regard, fitness exercise helps to distract your attention away from that cause of anxiety.

2. **Fitness exercise helps to prevent and relieve stress** – one of the leading causes of stress is anxiety. When anxiety is prevented and relieved, stress dies out. On the other hand, stress can be caused by the build-up of stress hormones which may be due to monotony, boredom, anger, etc. When you go fitness exercise, monotony, boredom, and anger dissipate just as anxiety does.

3. **Fitness exercise helps to relieve the symptoms of ADHD** – fitness exercise improves one's mood, motivation, memory, and concentration - the very remedies of ADHD (Attention Deficit Hyperactivity Disorder).

4. **Fitness exercise helps to relieve PTSD and trauma** – studies have indicated that, by focusing your body while fitness exercise, you help to jumpstart your

nervous system from some kind of 'stuck' which is essential in helping you get out of post-traumatic immobilization stress such as that experienced during PTSD (Post-Traumatic Stress Disorder) and trauma.

5. **Fitness exercise triggers the 'feel-good effect'** – scientific studies have proven that fitness exercise helps to trigger the release of endorphin hormones which creates a feeling of happiness and euphoria. Further studies have shown that this can have an effect as great as swallowing an antidepressant pill which is used for treating depression. Fitness exercise can also alleviate symptoms amongst clinically depressed persons. The good thing is that, unlike anti-depressant pills, fitness exercise has no side-effects.

6. **Fitness exercise helps to prevent cognitive decline** – the more we age, the higher is our rate of loss of memory and thinking ability. This is a natural cognitive decline. However, through fitness exercise, we can slow down this pace and even

prevent the early onset of it. Which, in essence, simply means by fitness exercise we can live a longer quality life.

7. **Fitness exercise helps to sharpen memory** – with fatigue, stress, and anxiety our memory gets strained and clogged up. When we run, we help to release this strain and clogging such that our memory regains its activeness which boosts our ability to remember things. This boosts our work, studies, and overall wellbeing.

8. **Fitness exercise increases brain power** – recent studies have found out that fitness exercise helps to increase the amount of brain-derived cells in the body which are associated with improved mental acuity, higher thinking capacity, and better learning. Further studies have indicated that athletes have faster response time sudden situations due to higher levels of alertness. This becomes so important in

avoiding accidents and handling emergencies, be they at home or workplace.

9. **Fitness exercise increases circulation (of air and blood) in the brain** – fitness exercise increases heart rate and intake of oxygen. These two actions help to boost blood circulation in the brain while at the same time improving the oxygen intake in the brain.

10. **Fitness exercise helps to control addiction** – fitness exercise has been known to prevent addiction in two ways. First, it denies you that idle time that you will feel like utilizing by engaging in the consumption of addictive substances such as smoking and drinking. Secondly, fitness exercise helps to reset the circadian clock to its proper functioning by making you tired enough to sleep during normal hours. It is known that addiction, more so, alcoholism disrupts this circadian rhythm thus making alcoholics stay long hours without sleep

which in turn pushes them to drink more to get rid of boredom.

11. **Fitness exercise increases brain relaxation** – after fitness exercise, you get physically fatigued. This condition of fatigue triggers your muscles to relax during resting. When muscles are relaxed, the metabolic activity goes down which helps the brain to relax.

12. **Fitness exercise boosts self-esteem** – runners are some of the most optimistic people around the world. In fitness exercise, you set targets and milestones to achieve. On the other hand, when anxiety and stress are relieved, you no longer have depressed moods and feeling low. This boosts your self-esteem, self-confidence, and vigor to tackle challenges just as you tackle your fitness exercise endeavor.

13. **Fitness exercise helps to boost sleep thus helping to remedy sleeping disorders** – when do fitness workout, you become physically tired after it. This

triggers the brain to push you to sleep mode so that you can have some good rest, especially during night time. This helps to remedy some sleeping disorders such as insomnia.

14. **Fitness exercise boosts mental creativity** – one of the things that tire the brain and thus make it less creative is anxiety, stress, monotony, and boredom. When you go fitness exercise, all these are overcome thus sparing the brain energy to be utilized towards creative endeavors.

15. **Fitness exercise helps to prevent brain tumor** – fitness exercise boosts your blood circulation, cell regeneration, immunity, neutralization of free radicals in the body, detoxification through sweat and urine thus sparing your cells the harmful elements that can distort them leading to the cancerous formation. Thus, fitness exercise helps to prevent the onset of brain tumors among many other types of cancers.

No people in their sane minds would wish to deny themselves of these 15 key benefits that result in longer, healthier and happier lives. You too cannot deny yourself of these immense benefits. If you've stopped fitness exercise or haven't been doing so, this is the time to wake up and hit the road on your feet. You will start experiencing instant positive changes in your life. Do it today, if not now!

Why Exercises are Important for Stress Relief

Although relieving stress is an all-encompassing endeavor comprising of physical, mental, psychological, emotional and spiritual endeavors, exercises do play a great role.

Exercises are important for stress reduction in the following ways;

- Release of helpful chemicals in the brain that helps to keep you off the stress. Exercises trigger your brains to release endorphins or "happy hormones" which frees you from stressful thoughts.

- Distraction from the cause of stress. When you are actively engaged in exercises, you disrupt dangerous thought patterns that bring up stress thus experiencing stress-free moments.

- Warms and relaxes cold, tight muscles and tissues which contributes to tension.

- It helps to reduce the rate of cognitive decline and its associated stress.

- It helps to avoid common health conditions that are known to aggravate stress levels. Such health conditions include high blood pressure, obesity, depression, stroke, osteoporosis, diabetes, dementia, Alzheimer's, Parkinson's disease and various forms of cancer including breast cancer, colon cancer, and lung cancer.

- Boosts your immunity system thus warding off most diseases that would otherwise bring worries and stress either to you or your loved ones.

- It makes you better at social engagements, especially when the exercises are carried out on a teamwork basis. Social engagements help you to get the necessary social and psychological support which prevents you from falling into unnecessary worries and build-up of stress.

- Boosts your moods thus helping you keep off dangerous emotional stress.

Simple Everyday Exercises that You Can Do to Relieve Stress

Aerobic versus Anaerobic exercises

Aerobic exercises are those exercises that need oxygen to burn fat and carbohydrates to release energy while doing them. This is primarily because they are long and not so intensive such as to inhibit regular oxygen flow into and out of your lungs.

Anaerobic exercises are the polar opposite of aerobic exercises. They are those exercises that do not need oxygen flow into and out of your lungs in order to burn fat and carbohydrates to release energy while doing them. This is because they are primarily short and highly intensive such that it is difficult to have regular oxygen flows while undertaking them.

Why aerobic exercises?

Aerobic exercises are commonly referred to as cardio exercises. This simply means that they relate to the heart functions. Aerobic exercises are important in exercising your heart and lungs.

The following are key benefits of aerobic exercises;

- They strengthen respiratory muscles thus enabling you to improve your oxygen intake capacity which is important for your well-functioning metabolism and stress release.

- They strengthen and boost the capacity of heart muscles which improves its pumping efficiency thus mitigating against any chance of dangerously resting heart rates. This contributes to improved oxygen and blood circulation into the brain thus helping to relieve stress accumulation.

- Boost the buildup, accumulation, and capacity of red blood cells thus facilitating the transportation of oxygen into the brains which safeguard your brain from stress.

- Boosts mental health, improves cognitive capacity, reduces stress and wards off serious mental conditions such as depression, Alzheimer and Parkinson's disease.

Why anaerobic exercises?

Anaerobic exercises are commonly referred to as endurance exercises or muscle strengthening exercises. They are important in exercising your muscles to enable you to better perform aerobic exercises.

The following are key benefits of anaerobic exercises;

- They tone down your body thus enabling you to have lean muscle mass.

- They enable you to burn fat and calories that saving you from risks of obesity which is a known aggravator of stress.

- Boosts the capability of your body to consume oxygen during your aerobic exercises which is important in ensuring that your brain doesn't easily get fatigued and eventually stressed up due to lack of adequate oxygen supply in the bloodstream.

- Contributes to lean and massive muscle tissues which increase your metabolism as they require your body to burn more calories to sustain their state thus helping you in your fight against obesity and eventually stress.

- Since anaerobic exercises depend on stored glycogen to provide required energy, this triggers your body to store more glycogen for anaerobic needs thus boosting your energy levels.

- Increased consumption of glycogen during anaerobic exercises lowers your blood sugar levels. Sugar is known to be a dangerous trigger of stress. Thus, when the sugar level in the blood is regulated, stress is relieved.

- Improved joint protection is guaranteed by your muscle mass and strength. Thus, anaerobic exercises that directly contribute to improved muscle mass and strength also directly contributes to improved joint protection. This helps you avoid the stress that emanates from painful injuries.

- Increased bone density and strength. Decreased bone density and strength has been the greatest contributor to osteoporosis. Osteoporosis is a major cause of stress especially for women in old age.

- Overcome soreness during exercises or intense physical activity. One disadvantage of aerobic exercise is the accumulation of lactic acid in the body. Anaerobic exercises boost your body's tolerance to lactic acid and thus decreasing soreness as a result of exercising.

The need for indoor exercises

Indoor exercises are important for the following key reasons;

- You are able to carry on with your stress relief exercises even at night or when the weather conditions are bad such as heavy rains, storm, scorching sunlight, etc.

- You are able to carry out your stress-busting exercises even when you have no access to open fields within reach.

- You can easily switch between them and other regular house chores or carry them with some other house chores concurrently.

- You can easily make the exercises as part of your family's fun activity.

The need for outdoor exercises

Outdoor exercises are important for the following key reasons;

- You are able to experience maximum exposure to fresh oxygen supply while carrying out aerobic exercises.

- You are able to carry out exercises in a team without space limitations.

- The outdoor environment helps to absorb attention away from your own stressful inner thoughts.

- You can be able to take advantage of nature (such as tree branches, fallen logs, tree stumps, rocks, hills, mountains, rivers, etc) and infrastructure (such as parks, park benches, paths, etc) to advance your exercises.

Balancing the act

To get the best out of your stress-relieving exercise regimen, you need to balance between indoor and outdoor, aerobic and anaerobic exercises in order to optimize the resultant outcome.

Strategies to Help You Get Moving for Long

The following strategies can go a long way in helping you succeed in your endeavor to relieve your stress;

A. Consider mental exercises

Sometimes it is better to play mental games, such as poker, draft, crossword puzzle, scrabble, etc with friends than idle alone. Idling easily makes you start reflecting on the past or uncertain future rather than the present moment. Thinking of past regrets or future worries breeds stress.

B. Consider social exercises

Get involved in social sporting endeavors such as beach volleyball, tennis, rugby, football, etc. These will enable you to get enough support to prevent and overcome stress.

C. Blend your exercises to get the best outcome

Have a mixture of exercises to have the best outcome. Indoor and outdoor exercises; aerobic and anaerobic exercises; individual and team exercises, etc helps you to optimize on your stress relief.

D. Consider your diet

Diet is a very important complement to your exercise for stress relief. Some nutritional deficiencies are known to aggravate stress conditions. Thus, it is also important to consider stress relieving diets as part of your program.

E. Consider your all-round wellness

Have all-round wellness encompassing physical, mental, emotional, social, psychological and spiritual wellbeing. Lack of balance and harmony in your life is by far the ultimate cause of stress.

F. Do plan

Plan your stress relief endeavor such that you can keep routine, discipline, measurement, feedback and control into proper perspective. This will enable you to optimize your outcome.

G. Do religiously execute your plan

A lot of stress comes from not being able to discipline yourself enough to successfully undertake your life endeavors. Thus, failure to keep discipline in your stress relief plans could be counterproductive. Execute your plans religiously so that you find no unjustifiable reason to veer off the track.

H. Do reward yourself

You must set challenging yet achievable milestones in your stress relief plan and reward yourself whenever you achieve your plan. This will boost your morale and make your brain release more endorphins to make you feel good and happy.

Chapter 11: Recovering and Rejuvenating Your Mental Energy through Mindfulness Meditation and Yoga

Mindfulness meditation, or even meditation as a whole, has gained tremendous scientific recognition for its ability to relieve anxiety, stress, and depression – the three key symptoms of depleted mental energy.

In this chapter, we are going to consider how empaths can recover and rejuvenate their mental energy through mindfulness meditation and yoga.

Mindfulness Meditation to rejuvenate your mental energy

What is mindfulness?

Mindfulness is a state of being actively conscious to the moment of now in an open, caring and conscious way that is free from judging.

What is meditation?

Meditation is the process of bringing yourself back to a state of being by which your self-awareness is optimized. When you meditate, you are able to stop following the maps that have been ingrained into your mindset to enable you to carry out daily routines. In meditation, you are able to reconnect with your inner being and reflect from within.

What is the relationship between mindfulness and meditation?

Meditation is the action or practice that is designed to achieve mindfulness. Mindfulness is the achieved state brought about by meditation.

Thus mindfulness meditation is a kind of meditation intended to achieve mindfulness.

Why practice mindfulness meditation?

Mindfulness meditation has immense benefits in your wholesome life. It is extremely difficult to quantify these benefits as they are immense and at times immeasurable. Nonetheless, we can list some of these benefits which are broadly classified under the following categories;

- Mental and psychological benefits
- Physical and physiological benefits
- Social, emotional and spiritual benefits

The Goal of Practicing Mindfulness Meditation

The goal of practicing mindfulness is to experiencing life now in its fullness. Experiencing life in its fullness means;

- Living it fully in the present without apportioning part of this living neither to the past nor the future

- Being consciously aware of life as you live it such that no part of it goes to waste as you hold attachments to the past or develop attachments to the future

- Exposing yourself to fully experience the moment of now without undue reservations

- Experiencing every moment without attaching your identity to it. When you attach your identity to the moment, it goes into the past with you.

The Key ingredients of Mindfulness Meditation

1. Being free to experience the moment of now
2. Being free from judgment
3. Being free from attachment

Being free to the moment of now -Being free to the moment of now simply means that you apply the fullness of your conscious awareness to the moment of now. Being free to experience the moment of now allows you not to apportion some of your consciousness to what happened yesterday. Similarly, being free to the moment of now allows you not to apportion some of your consciousness to what ought to happen tomorrow. Being free and present to the moment of now means that you are neither controlled by yesterday nor tomorrow. It is only by being free to experience the moment of now that you can fully be present now. Otherwise, you will partially be present now which is only but a condition of sub-optimality.

Being free from judgment - Being free from judgment simply means you do not attach your opinions to the happenings of now but act as an independent observer to the happenings without disturbing them by your preferences and prejudices. Opinions, preferences, and prejudices are based on judgments using criteria from past experiences and hence are already stale and thus cannot apply to this moment of freshness. These judgments are like plagues that start attacking the freshness of now and thus turning it into decays of yesterday. A life lived in fullness is a life lived to the freshness of being present in the moment of now.

Being free from attachment - Being free from attachments is the greatest of all freedoms. Being free from attachments doesn't necessarily mean that you are not attached. It simply means that you have power over those attachments such that they do not enslave you. Unnecessary attachments are the clinging that causes you pain. They are like anchors to a ship that has already embarked. The result is a constant struggle to move on without any motion being experienced but stagnation.

Being free from attachments means that your power to attach and power to detach are fully within your control. When you have the power to attach without a countering power to detach, you become a slave to attachments. Examples of situations when you become a slave to attachments are addictions. Another scenario where you lose power to detach is when you still cling to a failed relationship that your consciousness keeps telling you that you ought to detach. In essence, you are addicted to that relationship just as you would be addicted to Cigarettes, Cocaine, Heroin and all sorts of addictive drugs.

The Key Benefits of Mindfulness Meditation

Mindfulness has unlimited benefits that cut across all spheres of life. The overall key benefits of mindfulness are;

- Mindfulness meditation heightens your level of awareness

- Mindfulness meditation enables you to be fully present in the moment of now

- Mindfulness meditation enables you to learn to distinguish between you and your thoughts

- Mindfulness meditation enables you to become more connected to your being, the nature of beings and the nature of things.

- Mindfulness meditation enables you to be in harmony with your being, the nature of beings and the nature of things

- Mindfulness meditation enables you to develop self-acceptance which yields self-contentment and self-compassion

- Mindfulness meditation enables you to learn that life is dynamic and thus everything changes. Hence thoughts and feelings come and go.

- Mindfulness meditation enables you to experience calmness and peacefulness

- Mindfulness meditation enables you to experience more balance in your emotions and reactions thus enabling you to be free from the chaos of emotional spikes and outbursts

- Mindfulness meditation enables you to become aware of what you are subconsciously trying to avoid and thus be able to unearth and confront your fears

The key reasons as to why you ought to practice mindfulness

The key reasons as to why you ought to practice mindfulness are immense. Practicing mindfulness enables you to;

1. cultivate contentment
2. build your self-confidence
3. master your own mind
4. live in the moment of now
5. gain the 'power to be me'

Cultivate contentment - Contentment is a condition that exists when you are fully aware of the present. It is an awakening that sees the irrelevance of yesterday and tomorrow to your enjoyment of the present.

Build your self-confidence - Without self-confidence, you live in fear. Fear is derived from past experiences being applied to the present and or extrapolated into the future. Self-confidence is a condition that exists when you feel adequate to fully experience the moment of now.

Master your own mind - You need to master your mind. Without mindfulness, this would be such a daunting task. Without mindfulness, your mind is likely to depose you and become your master.

Live in the moment of now - To live in the moment of now is to relieve yourself of the two unwarranted loads - 'yesterday' and 'tomorrow'.

Living in the moment of now makes you light enough to walk in the present as it unveils.

Gain the 'power to be me' - Your mind has a map that has been modeled by culture, traditions and past experiences. This map doesn't allow you the freedom to experience an uncharted path but a predetermined path. Yet, you can never have the 'power to be me' if you are directed by other people via a mind map created through their culture, traditions, and teachings. You have to be liberated from your mind to experience this.

The key objectives as to why you ought to practice mindfulness

The objectives of practicing mindfulness vary from person to person. However, irrespective of your situation, the following are key objectives;

1. To raise one's awareness
2. To rise above the control of your mind

3. To experience a fulfilling life

4. To be happy

Yoga to Reinvigorate Your Energy Flow (Kundalini Yoga)

The vitality of life is composed of energy flows. Energy is required to breathe and think. When this energy is frustrated, both breathing and thinking too become frustrated.

The following are Yoga Poses that can help you reinvigorate your energy flows so that you can have sufficient power to liberate your mind and unclog your air flows;

1. Half Spinal Twist Pose

2. Spinal Flex Pose

3. Grasshopper Pose

4. Back Relaxation Pose

5. Big Toe Pose

6. Bow Pose

7. Cat-Cow Pose

8. Camel Pose

9. Cobra Pose

10. Plow Pose

11. Boat Pose

12. Fish Pose

Half Spinal Twist (Ardha Matsyendrasana)

In Sanskrit Ardha stands for Half; Matsya stands for Fish and Indra stands for the ruler. Thus, the pose is otherwise known as Half King of Fish.

Posture illustration:

Anatomical priorities :

- Spine
- Nervous system
- Back
- Abdomen
- Limbs

Therapeutic focus:

- spine
- nervous system
- back

abdominal muscles

Posture type: Spinal Twist

Duration: 3 – 5 minutes

Performance Instructions:

1. Start with a Seated Staff Pose

2. Bend your left leg and position its heel beside the right hip

3. Place the right leg over the left knee

4. Position the left hand on the right knee and the right hand behind your back

5. Twist your waist, shoulders, and neck in sequence to the right and glance over the right shoulder

6. Keep your spine straightened up

7. Stay into this position and make deep long inhalations and exhalations

8. Unfurl your Pose back to Seated Staff Pose by starting with the right hand, followed by the waist, then the chest and finally the neck.

9. Repeat steps (2) to (8) but beginning with the other side.

10. Breathe out and relax.

Therapeutic Benefits:

- Streamlines and strengthens the spine
- Opens the chest, heart and lung spaces thus increasing oxygen absorption and blood circulation
- Strengthens the back and abdominal muscles
- Stimulates the nervous, reproductive and digestive systems.

- Relieves sciatica

- It calms the brains thus helping to reduce stress and anxiety

Precaution:

- Avoid it if you have hip, back and shoulder injury

Recommendation:

- Start from Seated Staff Pose.

Spinal Flex (camel ride)

This is a yoga exercise targeting mainly your lower spine and middle back. It helps to streamline your spine and boost circulation while relieving stress and anxiety.

Posture illustration:

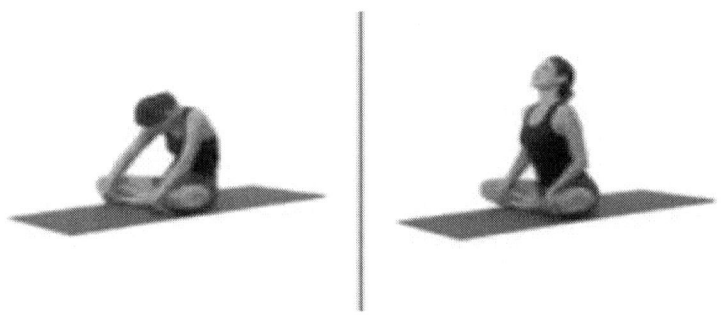

Anatomical priorities :

- Spine
- Nervous system
- Back
- Abdomen
- limbs

Therapeutic focus:

- spine

- nervous system
- back
- abdominal muscles

Posture type: Spinal Flex

Duration: 3 – 5 minutes

Frequency: 108 or more

Performance Instructions:

1. Sit in an Easy Pose (Sukhasana)
2. Hold your hands on your ankles
3. Flex the spine forward with your head stiffly straight and shoulders relaxed as you breath in deeply fast
4. Relax your spine as you exhale
5. Make as many repetitions as possible.

Therapeutic Benefits:

- Streamlines and strengthens the spine
- Strengthens the back and abdominal muscles
- Relieves sciatica
- It calms the brains thus helping to reduce stress and anxiety

Precaution:

- Avoid it if you have back and spine injury

Recommendation:

- Start from Easy Pose

Salabasana (Locust/Grasshopper Pose)

Salabasana is a combination of two Sanskrit words 'Salaba' meaning 'locust' and 'asa

na' meaning Pose. Thus, grasshopper pose.

Posture illustration:

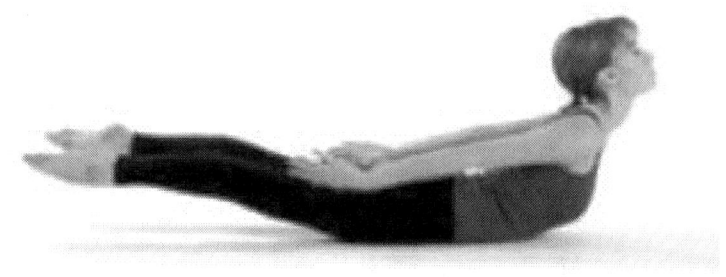

Anatomical priorities :

- Spine
- Nervous system
- Back
- Abdomen
- Limbs

Therapeutic focus:

- spine
- nervous system
- back abdominal muscles

Posture type: Grasshopper Pose

Duration: 3 – 5 minutes

Frequency: 2-3 times

Performance Instructions:

1. Lie down on your belly and stretch out your legs behind you with your feet tops pressing against the mat, your arms beside your torso and palms facing down.

2. Lift your thighs towards the sky as you firm your legs.

3. Engage your core as you draw your tailbone towards your heels and root your pubic bone into the mat

4. On your inhalation, lift your head, chest, arms, hands, feet, and legs off the ground as high as possible.

5. Keep your chest lifted up as you widen across your collarbone. Push your shoulder blades into your back ribs and extend them away from each other. Engage your back muscles while trying to release your glute muscles.

6. Keep your back elongated as your eye gaze point in the same direction as your sternum

7. Hold onto this position for one minute

8. To end, slowly exhale as you release your body to the mat.

Therapeutic Benefits:

- Strengthens and streamlines the upper and lower back
- Strengthens and streamlines the limbs

- Strengthens the back and abdominal muscles
- It opens the chest, shoulders, neck, and lungs.
- Boosts abdominal organs
- Improves overall body posture and flexibility
- Stimulates the nervous systems.
- It calms the brains thus helping to reduce stress and anxiety

Precaution:

- Avoid it if you have hip, back and shoulder injury

Recommendation:

- Focus on the length of your spine
- Rotate your thighs inwardly by turning your big toes towards each other.
- Draw your pelvis firmly into the mat
- Keep your buttocks soft but firm

Avasana (back-relaxation pose)

Savasana is a derivative of two words in Sanskrit "sava" meaning "corpse" and "asana" meaning pose. Savasana is considered the most important pose in Yoga.

Posture illustration:

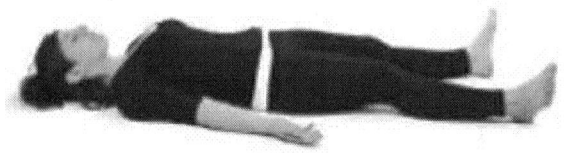

Anatomical priorities :

- Spine
- Back
- chest
- Nervous system

Therapeutic focus:

- Nervous system
- Respiratory system
- Cardiovascular system

Posture type: Back relaxation position

Duration: 5 - 30 minutes

Frequency: 2 – 3 or more per day

Performance Instructions:

1. Lie on your back with your legs straight

2. Lift up your pelvis slightly to push your tailbone away towards your legs so as to comfortably position your lower back and then rest your pelvis to the ground.

3. Let your legs feel natural and evenly straightened and your groin naturally relaxed.

4. Raise your hands straight up in the air above your face while slightly uplifting

your shoulders and adjusting them so that the shoulder blades spread evenly flat on the surface you ease the shoulders away from your neck and as your back ribs naturally expand.

5. Align your hands to comfortably rest astride at 45 degrees from your torso as your collarbone and chest naturally expand to follow up on the alignment. Make your palms look upwards to ease out circulation to your chest and shoulders.

6. Elongate the back of your neck by lightly pushing your chin towards your chest.

7. Grasp a slow deep inhalation to the lung's full capacity.

8. Gradually exhale letting your body relax and rest to the ground.

9. Be still as you relax setting your mind free. Let your eyes relax into their sockets as your tongue, cheek, jaw and forehead muscles soften out.

10. Focus inwards as giving more attention to your breath as you watch your body relax.

11. Take about 5 to 30 minutes of relaxation depending on how comfortable you feel.

12. To end your pose, exhale gradually and deeply as you fold your torso to bring your chest onto your knees and make a lengthwise pendulum swing using your back as spring. Alternatively, swing from left to right and back. Push yourself to a Seated Staff Pose and just relax to feel the stillness and calmness of your mind.

Therapeutic Benefits:

- Relaxes the nervous systems
- Relieves stress, anxiety, and depression
- Lowers blood pressure
- Decreases muscle tension
- Relieves fatigue
- Relieves insomnia

- Boosts energy levels

Precaution:

- If you are uncomfortable lying on your back, try to use some support
- If you are pregnant, use raised support to raise up your head and upper back

Recommendation:

- The final relaxation is crucial to a calmed mind. Give it sufficient time

Big Toe Pose (Padangusthasana)

Padagusthasana is a Sanskrit compound word combining three words 'pada' meaning 'foot', 'angustha' meaning 'big toe' and 'asana' meaning 'pose'. When combined it brings 'big toe pose'.

Posture illustration:

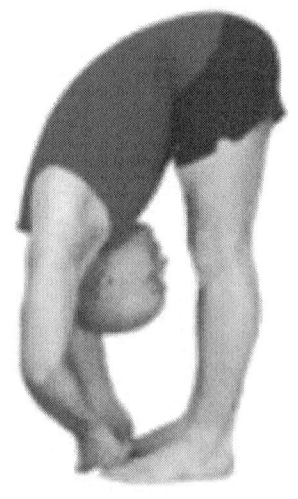

Anatomical priorities :

- legs
- thighs
- shoulders

Therapeutic focus:

- hamstring
- hips
- ankles
- shoulders

Posture type: Grasshopper Pose

Duration: 3 – 5 minutes

Frequency: 5 – 10 a day

Performance Instructions:

1. Start with a Mountain pose (Tadasana)
2. Position your feet to parallel to each other at a hip-width astride
3. Exhale as you bend forward
4. Hold the big toes with the first two fingers and a thumb for each hand on each leg

respectively in such a manner that the fingers and the thumbs are holding the big toes around.

5. Make a deep inhalation as you press the feet down and stretch the thighs up.

6. Pull the arms up and lengthen the sides forward to create a distance between the legs and the hands as both arms and legs are stretched. Open your chest and gaze out.

7. Exhale as you pull up on the toes as such to let the elbows protrude sideways of the legs as they bend.

8. Draw the chest downwards to flow together with the sides of the trunk

9. Hold the position for several breaths

10. To unfurl this pose, inhale and repeat as you repeat steps (2) to (8) above in reverse.

Therapeutic Benefits:

- Stretches, streamlines and strengthens legs and ankles

- It stretches and streamlines the hamstrings leading to gently open the shoulders, arms, and hips.

- It greatly boosts your sense of balance thus leading to greater focus and better concentration which helps to relieve stress and anxiety

Precaution:

- Avoid it if you have hip, back, shoulder and ankle injury

- Avoid it if you are in advanced stages of pregnancy

Recommendation:

- Keep your spine straight and shoulders relaxed

- Focus on the stretch, not the lift
- Take it gradually

Bow Pose (Dhanurasana)

In Sanskrit, 'Dhanu' means 'bow' and 'asana' means 'pose'.

Posture illustration:

Anatomical priorities :

- Back
- spine
- chest
- abdomen

Therapeutic focus:

- back
- abdominal muscles

- limb muscles

reproductive organs

Posture type: Back relaxation position

Duration: 30 seconds

Frequency: 5 – 7 at a time

Performance Instructions:

1. Lie on your stomach with your feet hip-width astride and your arms beside your torso

2. Bend your knees and hold your ankles with your hands

3. While breathing in, lift up your chest off the ground while pulling your legs and back up

4. Look straight forward and keep your pose stable as you observe your breath.

5. Take long breaths as you keep this pose

6. After 30 seconds, end the pose by exhaling as you gradually lower your chest and legs to the ground.

7. Release the ankles and relax.

8. Repeat steps (2) to (7) for 5 to 7 repetitions.

Therapeutic Benefits:

- Stretches, streamlines and strengthens abdominal muscles
- Tones limb muscles
- Opens chest, shoulders, and neck
- Relieves constipation and menstrual discomfort
- Helps to relieve renal disorders
- Stimulates reproductive organs
- Relieves fatigue, stress, and anxiety

Precaution:

- Avoid if you have chronic back problems, hernia, blood pressure, headache and migraine
- Avoid if you are in advanced stages of pregnancy
- Avoid if you have recently undergone abdominal surgery

Recommendation:

- Do it when your stomach is not full.

Cat-Cow Pose (Marjaryasana-Bitilasana)

Even cats and cows do yoga! This pose is inspired by watching how the cats and cows do stretch. In Sanskrit, 'marjari' means 'cat' and 'asana' means pose thus Cat Pose. Also in Sanskrit, 'Bitila' means 'cow' thus Bitilasana means Cow Pose. A cat-cow pose is a combination of these two poses that complement one another.

Posture illustration:

Anatomical priorities :

- Spine
- Back
- shoulders
- Wrists

Therapeutic focus:

- Spine
- Nervous system
- Digestive system
- Shoulders
- Wrists

Posture type: Cat-Cow Pose

Duration: 15 - 30 minutes

Frequency: 15 – 20 reps

Performance Instructions:

1. Suspend your head, neck, and torso on your hands and knees

2. Position your hands shoulder-width apart and your knees hip-width apart

3. Fully spread your fingers with middle ones facing forward

4. Bring your back into a horizontal table-top like position

5. Gather and feel a neutral position whereby your front and back feel evenly anchored

6. Deeply inhale as you drop your belly towards the mat into a Cow Pose

7. Lift up your chest and chin and gaze up towards the sky

8. Stretch your shoulder blades to broaden across as you draw your shoulders away from your ears

9. As you exhale, pull your belly to your spine and bow out your back towards the sky to look like a cat stretching its back – thus Cat Pose

10. Fall the crown of your head towards the ground but don't push your chin to the chest

11. Deeply inhale as you gradually collapse your belly into Cow Pose and then exhale

as bow out your back into Cat Pose. Repeat this for about 15 times

12. Rest by sitting back on your heels with your torso straight upright.

Therapeutic Benefits:

- Flexes the spine
- Strengthens shoulders and wrists
- Tones the abdomen
- Boosts digestion
- Improves blood circulation
- Relaxes the nervous systems
- Relieves stress, anxiety, and depression
- Boosts energy levels

Precaution:

- Avoid it if you have chronic back/neck problems

- Avoid it if you are at advanced stages of pregnancy

Recommendation:

- Match your breath be in sync with your movements

Camel Pose (Ustrasana)

In Sanskrit, 'ustra' means 'camel' and 'asana' means 'pose'.

Posture illustration:

Anatomical priorities :

- Back
- spine
- chest
- abdomen

Therapeutic focus:

- back
- abdominal muscles

- limb muscles
- reproductive organs

Posture type: Camel Pose

Duration: 3 -5 minutes

Frequency: At least twice daily

Performance Instructions:

1. Kneel on a mat with your legs hip-width apart and place your hands on your hips with your thumbs pressed on the bony plate at the base of your spine. Internally twist your thighs, squeezing them against each other while maintaining your hips above your knees. Letting your knees to be in line with your shoulders while the sole of your feet facing upwards

2. deeply inhale to engage your lower belly as you extend your tailbone towards your pubis as if being pulled from the navel

thus creating space between your lower vertebrae

3. on subsequent inhalation, raise your sternum and push your elbows towards each other thus letting your rib cage to expand

4. Arch your back, keep your chest raised, your spine elongated as you drop your hands towards your heels and slide your palms over your feet till the arms get straight.

5. Press your palm's heels against your feet's heels while resting your fingers over the soles.

6. Raise up your shoulders to let the trapezius muscles between your shoulder blades to expand and thus cushion your cervical spine.

7. Subtly lower your head and neck and gaze at your nose's tip

8. Stay in this position of a couple of inhalations and exhalations

9. To end, breath out gradually, draw your chin towards your chest and place your hands to your hips with the thumbs on the sacrum. Use your hands to support your lower back as you engage your belly as you rise up slowly.

Therapeutic Benefits:

- Stretches, streamlines and strengthens abdominal muscles
- Boosts digestion
- improves the spine's flexibility and streamlines your posture
- Tones limb muscles
- Opens chest, shoulders, and neck
- Relieves constipation and menstrual discomfort

- Relieves fatigue, stress, and anxiety

Precaution:

- Avoid if you have chronic back problems and low blood pressure
- Avoid if you are in advanced stages of pregnancy
- Avoid if you have recently undergone abdominal surgery

Recommendation:

- Do it when your stomach is not full.
- Engage your breath to engender a calm, clear mind that boosts your inward focus to detect subtle sensations which may help you avoid unnecessary injuries or forced pose.

Cobra Pose (Bhujangasana)

In Sanskrit, 'Bhujang' means 'cobra/snake' and 'asana' means 'pose'.

Posture illustration:

Anatomical priorities :

- Back
- spine
- chest
- abdomen

Therapeutic focus:

- back, spine, shoulders

- abdominal muscles
- sciatica and asthma

Posture type: Cobra Pose

Duration: 3 – 5 minutes

Frequency: At least twice daily

Performance Instructions:

1. Lie on your belly face-down, your chin on the yoga mat, your legs stretched and a few inches apart with your toes flat on the mat.

2. Pull up your knee caps, squeeze your buttocks and thighs and press your pubic bone on the mat

3. Grasp a deep inhalation, slowly lift up your head, chest, and abdomen without engaging your hands while keeping your navel pinned on the mat

4. With your elbows close to your sides, lift your torso off the ground supported by your arms. Make sure that the torso weight is balanced on your arms

5. Drop your back and shoulders down as you push your chest forward. Push your chest further forward as you straighten your arms and streamline the rest of your abdomen to keep your buttocks, legs firm while pressing your pubic bone on the mat.

6. Hold this position and make 2-6 breathes

7. To exit the pose, breathe out and gradually lower your chest and head to the mat. Turn the head on one side and toss your hips from side to side to release any stress in the lower back

Therapeutic Benefits:

- Stretches, streamlines and strengthens abdominal muscles

- Tones limbs, shoulders, and buttocks
- Opens chest, lungs, shoulders and neck
- Relieves constipation and menstrual discomfort
- Relieves sciatica and asthma
- Stimulates reproductive organs
- Relieves fatigue, stress, and anxiety

Precaution:

- Avoid if you have chronic back problems, headache, and migraine
- Avoid if you are in advanced stages of pregnancy
- Avoid if you have recently undergone abdominal surgery

Recommendation:

- Do it when your stomach is not full.
- Don't overdo the backbend

Plow Pose (Halasana)

In Sanskrit, 'Hala' means 'plow' and 'asana' means pose thus Plow Pose.

Posture illustration:

Anatomical priorities :

- Back
- abs
- shoulders
- limbs

Therapeutic focus:

- Abs
- Back
- Shoulders
- Limbs
- Nervous system

Posture type: Plow Pose

Duration: 3 -5 minutes

Frequency: At least once a day

Performance Instructions:

1. Start by lying your back on a yoga mat with your legs stretched out and your arms by your sides and palms down.

2. Make a deep inhalation as you engage your abdominal muscles to catapult up your legs and hips towards the sky

3. Make your torso perpendicular to the ground. Straighten your legs and gradually lower them over your face at a 180-degree angle to the floor ahead with your legs straightened.

4. While your feet are resting comfortably on the floor, stretch your arms along the ground and interlace your fingers.

5. Press your upper arms firmly on the mat

6. Align your hips over your shoulders. Open up your toes and press the tops of your feet against the mat

7. Lift up your tailbone and push your inner groin deep into your pelvis.

8. Lift your chest to open the upper back as you simultaneously keep space between your chin and chest. Gaze down towards your cheek as you soften your throat.

9. Hold onto this pose for between 3-5 minutes.

10. To exit the pose, anchor your back with your hands and then gradually roll down one vertebra at a time, bending your knees if necessary.

Therapeutic Benefits:

- Strengthens the neck, shoulders, abs and back muscles
- Flexes the spine
- Tones the abdomen
- Stimulates the thyroid glands
- Boosts digestion
- Improves blood circulation
- Relaxes the nervous systems
- Relieves stress, anxiety, and depression
- Boosts energy levels

Precaution:

- Avoid it if you have chronic back/neck problems
- Avoid it if you are at advanced stages of pregnancy
- Avoid if you have diarrhea
- Avoid if you have high blood pressure

Recommendation:

- Match your breath be in sync with your movements
- Breath consciously throughout the pose
- Do not squeeze your buttocks as you keep your legs firm while straightening knees.

Boat Pose (Naukasana)

In Sanskrit, 'nauka' means 'boat' and 'asana' means 'pose'.

Posture illustration:

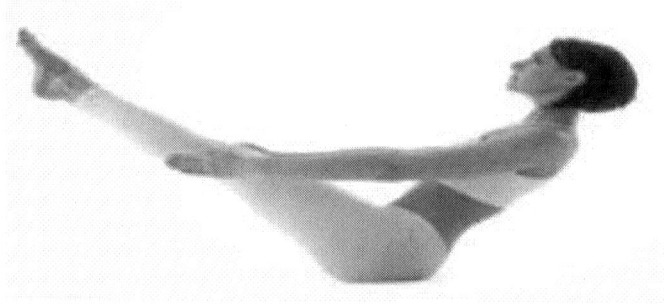

Anatomical priorities :

- Back
- Limbs
- abdomen

Therapeutic focus:

- back muscles
- abdominal muscles

- limb muscles

Posture type: Boat Pose

Duration: 4 – 8 Breaths

Frequency: At least twice daily

Performance Instructions:

1. From a Seated Staff Pose, bend your knees, bringing your feet to lay flat on the floor with legs together with your arms by your sides.

2. Take a deep inhalation and as you exhale, lean to form a 45-degree angle between your thighs and your belly. Draw your shoulders together to open the chest and lift it.

3. Gradually straighten your legs, kicking out through the heels lifting your legs up as high as your comfort allows.

4. Stretch your arms forward running parallel to the floor with palms facing the ground.

5. Maintain the pose as you keep on breathing deeply and deeply for about 4-8 breaths.

6. End by gradually exhaling, bending your knees and lowering your feet back to the floor.

Therapeutic Benefits:

- Stretches, streamlines and strengthens the back and abdominal muscles
- Tones limb muscles
- Relieves fatigue, stress, and anxiety

Precaution:

- Avoid if you have chronic back problems and low blood pressure

- Avoid if you are in advanced stages of pregnancy
- Avoid if you have heart problems and asthma

Recommendation:

- Do it when your stomach is not full.
- Engage your breath to engender a calm, clear mind that relieves stress, fatigue, and anxiety.

Fish Pose (Matsayasana)

In Sanskrit, 'matsaya' means 'fish' and 'asana' means 'pose'.

Posture illustration:

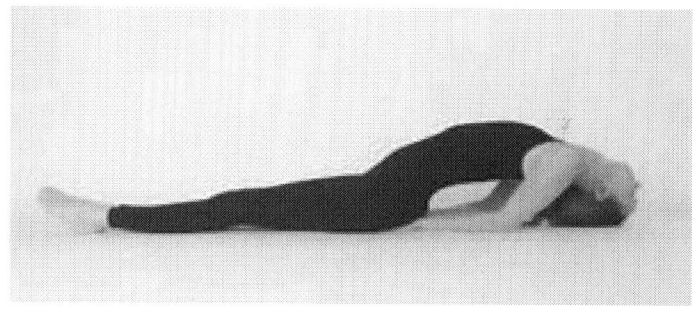

Anatomical priorities :

- Back
- spine
- chest
- abdomen

Therapeutic focus:

- back
- abdominal muscles
- limb muscles

Posture type: Fish Pose

Duration: 5-7 minutes

Frequency: At least once daily

Performance Instructions:

1. Lie on your back with your legs stretched and your arms beside your torso with palms facing down

2. While breathing in, press your forearms and elbows on your mat and lift up your chest to create an arch in your back.

3. Lift your torso and shoulder blades off the mat. Bend your head backwards letting the crown of your head touch the mat.

4. Lift your chest up from in between the shoulder blades.

5. Engage your thighs and legs by pressing them down on the mat

6. Hold on into this position for five deep breaths

7. To end, press your forearms firmly on the mat and lift up your head off the ground. Exhale gradually as you lower your head and torso to the mat. Pull your knees towards your chest, for 2-3 breaths and then extend your legs for rest.

Therapeutic Benefits:

- Stretches, streamlines and strengthens abdominal and intercostals muscles
- improves the spine's flexibility and streamlines your posture
- Opens chest, lungs, throat, shoulders, and neck
- Improves breathing and helps to remedy respiratory ailments
- Tones pituitary, pineal, and parathyroid glands
- Relieves constipation and menstrual discomfort
- Relieves fatigue, stress, and anxiety

Precaution:

- Avoid if you have chronic back problems and low blood pressure
- Avoid if you are in advanced stages of pregnancy
- Avoid if you have recently undergone abdominal surgery

Recommendation:

- Do it when your stomach is not full.
- Keep your neck comfortably extended without strain.
- Keep your legs actively engaged throughout the pose
- Don't put much weight on the head

PART III: MANAGING YOUR RELATIONSHIPS AND ENVIRONMENTS AS AN EMPATH

Overview

Empaths desire relationships with other human beings just like everyone else.

However, they differ from non-empaths on how they cultivate and nurture these relationships. More importantly, their level of sacrifice and commensurate benefit differs significantly from that of non-empaths. This makes it extremely important for empaths to manage their relationships in such a manner that matches sacrifices with benefits.

In this Part, we are going look at the workplace relationship as one of the most important relationships where empaths are likely going to be more disadvantaged on the cost-benefit scale.

More often than not, empaths find themselves more drained and draught in relationships and environments with strenuous social interactions. As we have seen before, while non-empaths are likely going to be charged up by vibrant social interactions, empaths are more likely to be discharged. Thus, it is important for empaths to learn how to survive in such socially strenuous environments... be it at work, social events, or intimate relationships.

Empaths, like other human beings, are greatly shaped up during their childhood. It is at this malleable stage that certain enduring characters are molded. However, it can become a big challenge when it comes to raising a child empath. There are likely going to be a lot of misunderstandings. And with these misunderstandings, there are likely going to be a lot of reactions from parents that may hurt, hinder, or inhibit the growth potential of an empath child and thus constrain the child's development. Many empaths suffer childhood trauma due to having been poorly mishandled by caregivers (especially parents) who did not understand their unique needs and treated them in a harsher or more hostile way in the belief that they were being 'abnormal' or 'too demanding of attention'.

Thus, managing relationships and environments is extremely important to the health and wellbeing of an empath – right from childhood to adulthood.

Chapter 12: How to Manage Your Work Environment and Boost Your Productivity as an Empath

It is inevitable that empaths, once at their productive age, will experience the work environment. Their sensitivity won't be muted simply because of work.

They will still carry with their nature, and personality as empaths at the workplace.

And just as empaths are frequently misunderstood at home and social environments, they too are misunderstood at the workplace. This calls for them to take greater responsibility towards managing their sensitivity such that it does not inhibit their productivity.

Naturally, empaths are more prone to procrastination than non-empaths, this is because they take their time thinking through before acting.

This procrastination can also have a negative impact on their punctuality and timekeeping. Sometimes, due to their mood swings, they may wake up some days with greater inertia than others. The higher the inertia, the less conscious it is to keep time. Lateness and absenteeism increase with inertia.

Previously, we've seen the impact of a cluttered environment on empaths. Empaths are extremely sensitive to their environment. They love the natural environment characterized by calmness and serenity.

Clutters, especially from unnatural objects can drain their energy and leave them more lethargic and highly sensitive.

To cope and create a conducive work environment where empaths can be more productive, it simply means that they have to give importance to decluttering, punctuality, and avoiding procrastination.

Declutter

A cluttered environment is an energy-sapping environment to an empath. Clutter saps energy from the empath thus causing the empathy to feel tired, irritated, worn out and confused.

A cluttered work environment lowers the empath's productivity. This can cause the empath's career to be frustrated as the bosses will consider the empath as a low-energy, and underserving of greater responsibility which comes with higher pay.

At worst, a cluttered environment can cause a strain in the relationship between the empath and fellow workmates. This is because of the empath's level of irritability soars, which means that the empath will become easily angered with just minimal provocation.

To declutter, the empath has to practice decluttering the workspace as a habit. This habit involves:

- Clearing the workstation and arranging things before the end of working hours – this will ensure that the empath will arrive the next day to a clean and organized work environment

- Clearing any pile-up soonest possible – an empath must avoid procrastination. Thus, the empath should embark immediately on any new assignment and attend to any incoming mail or document.

- Ensuring that, apart from the in-tray and out-tray, no documents are left scattered on the workstation

- Filing off documents that are not of immediate attention

- Tucking shoes and extra garment (such as a sweater, jacket, coat, etc) away from the workspace. While most offices have provision for shoe racks, few have provision for extra garments away from the workspace. It is good to vouch for a wardrobe so that extra garments can be kept aways for the workspace sight. If allowed, you can make a personal initiative of bringing a portable wardrobe to your workspace.

Keep time

Keeping time is extremely important to an empath. While some empaths are good timekeepers, some are not. Even those who are good timekeepers, they may experience periods of extremely low moods and dampened spirit such that they may end up arriving late.

Keeping time, just as decluttering is also an important habit.

The best time-keeping habit is to establish a routine.

Work routine

This will depend on your work schedule. While some schedules are flexible such that you have control over (if you are the self-employed or senior manager), others strictly tight such that you have no control over.

Whether your work routine is flexible or tight, it is important to consider the following:

- Do not skip your meals
- Engage in mobility exercises
- Have breaks to relax or refresh

Evaluating day-to-day plan

To evaluate is to weigh the outcome against targets/expectations as you carry out your implementation. It is the key part of managing success.

In our case, we implemented a day-to-day plan to increase productivity. Under evaluation, you will have to review the result of your implementation against set goals.

In managing success, you need to:

1. **Devise effective measurement standards** – Without measurement standards, it is impossible for you to be able to determine performance. There are various established standards for each particular task. Your experience can also be used to create a reasonable benchmark to which you can use to measure performance. The standard should be challenging but achievable.

2. **Develop an effective feedback reporting system** – once you have devised effective measurement standards, the next thing is to have an effective feedback reporting system. This system is akin to the quality control section within the production department. Every performance needs to be measured against the standard and the outcome reported immediately for quick action.

3. **Layout effective control mechanism** – a control mechanism is that mechanism

that helps to regulate performance such that any negative deviation is rectified.

Rewarding success /Reprimanding failure

A reward is a positive gain you get in making any given undertaking. In this case, when you achieve your target, you need to have some gain. Psychologists have discovered that reward triggers that 'feel good' part of the brain, which brings motivation to do more. Thus, rewarding yourself for your achieved target goes a long way in re-enforcing your motivation.

After evaluating the implementation of the day-by-day plan, the next thing is to reward yourself. Since this is part of structured productivity, this reward mechanism must also be structured.

The reward process encompasses the following steps:

1. **Establish** reward criteria – A reward criterion is a standard of attainment, which you have set such that achievement of that standard is rewarded. For example, if the target per day were jogging 3 miles a day, reward criteria would be, for every 3 miles of jogging achieved, you get to reward yourself with a good treat at the dining table.

2. **Create the most impacting reward mechanism** – a reward mechanism should be such it furthers your endeavor. For example, it is your desire while jogging to be fit and healthy. If you choose to take soda and junk foods at the dining table, this works against your endeavor – to stay fit and healthy. Thus, the food at the dining table should be such to help you boost your health. Such food should be a balanced diet of the natural whole meal.

3. **Endow the reward** – this is the actual giving of the reward. Having a great treat

at the dining table is the actual endowment of this reward.

In case you have experienced your very own cases of indiscipline such that they prevented you from successfully implementing your strategy, then, you need to reprimand yourself. This reprimand could take the form of:

- **Denying yourself the undue indulgences** - For example, if your target was jogging and you ended up in a bar. The next logical thing is to deny yourself from drinking at the bar.

- **Sacrificing other activities that are not important so that you can allocate more time to implementing your strategy** - Definitely taking alcohol at the bar is not as important as jogging. You may need to sacrifice this alcoholism for the sake of your jogging endeavor.

- **Keeping off a wrong company that deviates your attention from your goals** - If it is due to your friend's undue influence that you ended up in the bar despite your plan to avoid it, then, you would probably need to avoid your friend at such times you need to go jogging. That is if your friend is unwilling to go jogging with you.

- **Sacrificing resources from not-so-important ventures into implementing your strategy** - Spending money at the bar drinking simply means that you still have money that has not been allocated to priory areas. Commit that money to priority areas and you will not have much left to indulge it in alcohol.

Avoid procrastination

To overcome procrastination, it is extremely important that you first isolate the disease from its symptoms. When you treat the disease, the symptoms will naturally die. However, when you focus on treating the symptoms, you will get temporary relief while the disease remains uncured.

The following are key steps to overcoming procrastination:

1. Know what to do
2. Device action plan
3. Sharpen your resolve (tools and techniques)
4. Work on your mindset
5. Work on your habit

Know what to do

Knowledge is power. In the first section, we started off by embarking on knowledge of what procrastination is.

Let's explore knowing what to do in order to overcome procrastination. The first action is drawing the action plan itself.

The second important thing to do is to sharpen your resolve. It is a lack of determination and self-discipline that denies you focus on your goal. Thus, to be able to discipline yourself to focus on your goal, you must sharpen your resolve.

You must have realized that sharpening your resolve is mind-driven. Thus, you must work on your mind in order to succeed in sharpening your resolve. Your mind is the ground in which the tree of procrastination has its deep roots and derives its rich nutrients.

As we have seen in our first Section, procrastination is a habit. Like all other bad habits, procrastination begins in the mind. That's also the very place it must begin to be fought.

Sharpen your resolve

Sharpening your resolve requires you to regain your lost Willpower. Willpower is the innate ability to overcome inherent inertia. The greatest reason why procrastination happens is inertia.

Due to all other reasons, as we have discussed and shall continue to discuss, inertia brings that lazy reluctance to take action. You want to stand up but something seems to hook you onto the seat; you want to wake up but something seems to pin you down on the bed; you want to walk out but something seems to glue you onto the sofa.

You want to leave chatting on social media but something still nags and seems to shout 'wait for my next post!'; You seem to be arrested into a perpetual vicious cycle of waiting; You snap out from one cycle of waiting into the next awaiting cycle of waiting.

Your endless cycle of waiting cranks your willpower stamina making it not hit on when expected.

Willpower is that force that urges you to actualize your will. It keeps you focused on asserting your determined will regardless of the swaying from others, be it persuasive or coercive.

Key attributes of willpower are;

- Ability to postpone instant gratification
- Ability to overcome bursts of short-term emotional temptations in order to achieve long-term goals
- Ability to override destructive thoughts and impulses
- Self-control

Lack of willpower is due to many mind problems. However, the following are the most prominent causes of lack of willpower which you must confront in order to sharpen your resolve to end procrastination;

- Scarcity – perpetual scarcity makes it easy for people to lose their willpower. For example, those who wish to have a balanced diet may give up on their willpower if inadequate supplies of fruits and vegetables become perpetual.

- Money troubles - studies found out that money troubles have a strong negative psychological effect on the poor. Money troubles impair their thought-process as they slowly adapt to conditions that require less willpower to overcome. For example, it is a bad habit to pick from dumpsites, but money troubles may cause the poor to do that not because they don't know it is a bad habit, but their willpower has been lowered by money troubles.

- Constant decision-making – when people encounter many scenarios that require quick and constant decision-making, their mind gets worked-up and soon their willpower to continue making more decisions gets impaired.

- Stress – Stress is a result of overworked mental energy. Willpower consumes energy. Thus, when you are stressed, there is less energy available to your willpower.

Device action plan

An action plan is simply an executable plan. It is a plan that you have to carry out in order to achieve your goal. In this case, your goal is A LIFE FREE FROM PROCRASTINATION. Though, as we shall see later, this is still not yet the SMARTEST goal. But, for the time being, let it hold.

Life without a plan is the most chaotic of all lives that could ever be lived. You need not sweat out having complex plans that make your life harder than it ought to be or even much worse without it. To achieve unique and exceptional personal development, the goal of your life must be to make it EASIER.

An EASIER plan of action. This encompasses six critical components;

1. Envision
2. Assess
3. Strategize
4. Implement
5. Evaluate
6. Reward/Reprimand

Thus, EASIER is an acronym that stands for **E**nvision, **A**ssess, **S**trategize, **I**mplement, **E**valuate, and **R**eward.

Envision

To envision is to dream and visualize your dream. Once you have visualized your dreams, it becomes easy to idealize them. In envisioning, place yourself into that future you dream of and see your being in it.

Thus, to envision encompasses three critical steps;

- Dream
- Idealize
- Visualize
- Engender

Dream

Dreaming is the nursery from which ideas germinate. The seeds for these ideas are the imaginations. To dream is simply to tantalize imagination, entertain it and help it grow. With a dream big enough to be formidable, the next step is to idealize it.

Idealize

To idealize your dream is to map it out with clear points of reference. It is to refine and define it into a form that can be visualized.

Visualize

This is the core of envisioning. It is casting the map work of your dream into a grander scale with a clear perspective that can be easily assessed and actualized through strategy.

Visualizing is the process of creating a VISION. A vision is a state of being once your MISSION is accomplished and your GOAL achieved.

In this case, the vision is A HEALTHY AND WEALTHY LIFE RICHLY ENDOWED BY LOVING RELATIONSHIPS

Engender

To engender is to take ownership of your vision; to place it at the core of your heart; to humanize it; to make it capable of passion and effort. It is indeed to embrace your vision.

Assess

To assess is to make an analysis of what you envision, your capabilities required to achieve your vision, the ideas that come out of your mind in line with your vision, the prevailing circumstances, and situations.

The most significant tool for carrying out self-assessment or of that situation at hand is SWOT analysis.

SWOT analysis encompasses the following five elements;

- Your **S**trengths

- Your **W**eaknesses
- Your **O**pportunities
- Your **T**hreats

Procrastination requires a deep SWOT analysis so that you can be able to efficiently and effectively confront it.

SWOT your core inner variables

When you are making a SWOT analysis of yourself, the core variables that you would consider are those that form your inner being where your dreams, idealizations, visions and engenders are formed: Where their energizing power derive their source – right within your inner self.

The following are those core inner variables that you must SWOT about;

- Attitudes
- Habits
- Beliefs

- Fears

These are the very same variables that play a greater role in creating or ending procrastination.

Attitudes

An attitude is a learned tendency to evaluate matters in a certain manner. Such matters include people, objects, events, issues, etc.

Attitudes have three critical components;

- **Emotional component** – how matters under evaluation make you feel.

- **Cognitive component** – your thoughts and beliefs about matters at hand.

- **Behavioral component** – how your perception/evaluation influences your behavior.

Habits

A habit is a repetitive pattern of arriving at a certain outcome. This pattern could be a pattern of thoughts, actions or reactions.

Beliefs

A belief is a mental representation of an attitude towards the likelihood of a state being (or an outcome turning out) in a certain way.

Your mindset – the home to your inner variables

Your mindset is where your inner variables reside. You wholly depend on your mindset. Your mindset is the blueprint of your life.

Carry out a Self SWOT Analysis

SWOT analysis is a tool that helps you to evaluate your strengths, weaknesses, opportunities, and threats.

We've already seen SWOT in Chapter 3, above.

Strategize

To strategize is to set an action plan, or simply, plan of action to actualize your vision. This action plan must encompass your mission, goals, objectives, tasks, targets, and tactics.

In strategizing, you have to create a Planning Mindset that will help you set SMARTEST goals, break (decompose) your goals into functional domains (e.g. tasks, departments, milestones, etc) for easier handling. With SMARTEST goals established, the next thing is to implement your strategy.

- Create a planning mindset
- Set SMARTEST goals
- Decompose goals into functional domains
- Set manageable targets

Creating a planning mindset

Your mindset is the garden where your ideas grow and mature into plans. How healthy your ideas become depends solely on how you tend to this garden. Make it fertile and your ideas will become healthy and prosperous. You achieve this by working on your mindset.

Work on your mindset

A mindset is a set of beliefs, assumptions, and thoughts that make up one's mental attitude, habit, inclination or disposition which predetermines a person's perceptions and responses to situations, circumstances, and events.

Why is mindset such important?

Mindset is important because it is the point of reference to which you perceive and respond to events, circumstances, and situations. How you perceive things depends on your mindset. That's why many experts say that 'you see things as you are' and not necessarily as they are. This 'you are' is your mindset.

Mindset is the fertile ground upon which the seed of vision grows. How healthy and great your vision becomes solely depends on your mindset. A defective mindset will definitely yield a defective vision. A fixed mindset will yield a fixed vision. And thus, a transformational (growth) mindset will yield a transformational vision.

Vision: the place where your goal post ought to reside

Vision is a big picture of how things ought to be. Vision is what you would like to see once you have accomplished your mission and achieved your goal.

Why have a Vision?

The following are the key purposes of a Vision

1. It inspires you to take appropriate action
2. It helps you to communicate effectively with an inner compulsion
3. It helps you to marshal resources and rally people towards a common purpose
4. It empowers everyone who is inspired by it to achieve it.

The three essential qualities of your vision

A. Core Ideology

Core ideology is that set of ideals that inspire you to marshal your mind, heart, and sinew towards achieving a certain goal

There are two key elements;

1. **Core values** – these are the overriding principles that guide your life.

2. **Core purpose** – this is the key reason why you think you live.

B. Envisioned future
This is the picture of what you perceive to be your future.

C. Your attitude

This is your mental predisposition.

How to create a vision

1. Establish your core ideology
2. Break it down into distinct core values. Values are those essential qualities/principles that you believe are important in the way you live and work.
3. Blend your mission and core values to come up with an inspiring core purpose.

Mission: the key reason why you want to achieve your goals

A mission is the 'raison detre' or reason for the existence of your organization.

How to create a Mission

The sole purpose of a mission is to achieve a given set of goals.

Key qualities of a good Mission Statement

A good mission statement should;

1. Describe what your being is
2. Describe what your being seeks to do and why it seeks to do it
3. Be clear and concise
4. Be outcome-oriented
5. Be considerate of your key stakeholders – your family, your partner(s), friends, your colleagues, your employer, etc.

Salient questions that you must answer in your Mission

1. Who am I?
2. Why did I about?
3. What do I intend to do?
4. For whom do I intend to do it?
5. Why do I intend to serve my being the way I propose?
6. What distinguishes my vision from my current state?

7. How do I get my key stakeholders to understand my mission?

How to Develop your Mission Statement

1. Develop a compelling call
2. Clarify your goal
3. Capture and inspire your imagination
4. Manifest your core competencies
5. Motivate and inspire your commitment
6. Be realistic
7. Be specific, short, sharp and memorable

Setting SMARTEST goals

Without a goal, there is no achievement. It is like a body running without a head – such movement will be random, aimless and short-lived. A goal is an end that you pursue. It is a specific accomplishment that you desire at the end of your endeavor. It is the ultimate prize that you want to get out of your endeavor.

Why have a goal?

There are many benefits that accrue to your endeavor if it has a goal. A goal enables you to;

1. Have a direction
2. Be focused
3. Plan on what you can do to achieve your ultimate end
4. Be disciplined
5. Be able to measure your success

How do you create the SMARTEST goal?

A goal that will enable you to be able to achieve the best of your endeavor is one that is the SMARTEST of all goals.

For example, if you are in debt and you would like to get out of it;

> *Free myself from procrastination as quickly and as easy as possible but not later than three months by using a*

combination of necessary methods and techniques that would ensure I have regained my willpower and killed my identified bad habits from then henceforth so that I can enjoy a healthy and wealthy life richly endowed by loving relationships.

A SMARTEST goal must be;

Specific: a SMART goal must not be ambiguous but specific. A specific goal is that which answers the questions of what (free from procrastination); Why (so that I enjoy a healthy and wealthy live endowed by loving relationships); When (as quickly as possible but, not later than three months); Who (myself); Where (In my mindset) and How (by using a combination of necessary methods and techniques).

Measurable: a SMART goal must be measurable. You must be able to quantify your achievements. In this case, the achievement is killing my *identified*

habits (list them) as quickly as possible but not later than three months.

Achievable: a SMART goal must be attainable (achievable). You cannot expect to kill your identified bad habits if you have no willpower. You must work to strengthen your willpower.

Realistic: a SMART goal must be realistic. It must be such that you have both the ability and the will to achieve it. If either will or ability lacks, then, your goal is not realistic. Your will is expressed on how much you are ready to sacrifice to attain your goal. Your ability is what assets (methods, techniques, and skills) you have that you can use to execute your will.

Timely: a SMART goal must have a timeframe for its accomplishment. In our example, the timeframe is 'as quickly as possible, but no later than three months'. A goal that is not timely is not a SMART goal for its chances of being achieved cannot be defined.

Empowering: You are not a robot. You are driven not by electricity or fuel but by your inner desire to perform. The greatest drive that boosts your performance is motivation. A motivated person is an inspired person. An inspired person is an empowered person. A goal should be capable of empowering you to strive towards its achievement. To be self-empowered is to ignite the inner inspiration that motivates you to be on a self-drive towards the attainment of your set goals and objectives. To achieve this, first and foremost, you must have a transforming vision – a vision that you can easily peep through and see greatness. It must be such a stake that radically boosts your welfare – that makes you much better than you could ever imagine or dream of. In our case, HEALTH, WEALTH AND LOVING RELATIONSHIPS are motivating enough for you to desire to pursue them

Stimulating: A goal must be capable of being felt. It must touch and impact your heart as you think of it. You must be moved by it. You must hold it sentimentally. It must draw in the best of your emotional energy. In our case, ENJOY is such a powerful sensual feeling in our goal. It manifests that feeling of HEALTH, WEALTH and LOVING RELATIONSHIPS.

Transformational: A goal that is transformational is that which radically changes your status of things. One of the greatest causes of your lack of personal development is stagnation accompanied by eventual decay. Stagnation is costly, sometimes much more costly than motion. When there is a lack of newness and freshness into the way you do things, boredom and monotony sets in. Your rate of default in performance goes high. Your rate of accidents also rises due to your state of low levels of alertness. A transformational goal will push you from that stagnant pond of the status quo into a new stream of dynamism. In our case, HEALTH, WEALTH and LOVING RELATIONSHIPS are great transformations from the boring, monotonous state of procrastination.

Work on your habit

As we have seen previously, procrastination is a habit. You have to work on your habit so as to change it.

Daily habits to overcome procrastination

These daily habits include;

1. Mind habits
2. Behavioral habits
3. Lifestyle habits

Mind habits

- Meditate often – meditation helps to sharpen your focus so that you are able to get to the depth of the root cause of your procrastination.
- Be mindful – mindfulness helps to boost your self-awareness. Self-awareness is important in determining the root cause of your depleted willpower.
- Engender positivity – positivity motivates you to take beneficial action against procrastination
- Be compassionate – compassion inspires you to snap out of procrastination. It pushes you to overcome inertia and thus take actions that help to promote a greater good for everyone. This is extremely important in caring for your

own health and of others; building strong lasting bonds and creating real wealth.

Behavioral habits

- Smile unreservedly – a smile opens your inner being to the warmth of external radiation thus melting the solid ice of inertia within.
- Laugh often and much – laughing does what a smile does but on a grander scale.
- Take the challenge – every challenge has an opportunity to end procrastination. Every challenge you take is a victory over inertia.
- Embrace defeat wholeheartedly – fear of losing is one of the greatest motivational force behind procrastination. Embracing defeat wholeheartedly is not to attach yourself to the perception of loss but to the enjoyment of the game itself.
- Be gracious in your win – pride always comes before a fall. You cannot be in a forever state of win. There are times you will lose. Losing is simply parting with the old win so that a new win can become possible. It is not bad in itself

but a change that you deserve. When you become proud while making a win, you are bound to feel humiliated when you lose. Graciously accepting your win allows you to lose without humiliation. Humiliation is one of the main fears that make people procrastinate. They fear to lose what they already have. Yet, you cannot become productive, and you cannot achieve your best if you fear to lose. Losing is not a failure but an opportunity for a new chance of winning.

Lifestyle habits

- Eat well – eating affects your mind. What affects your mind has an effect on your procrastination. Low glycemic diet, lean proteins, nuts, fresh fruits and vegetables, and omega 3 fatty acids are great for your mind as they are great for your brain. Sometimes, procrastination is caused by low brain energy.
- Be active – carry out chores that allow your body mobility. Exercise often. Play outdoor sports and games. This way, your brain

becomes excited and as such, overcoming inertia becomes a reflex action that doesn't necessarily require your conscious input.

- Balance activity – don't dwell on one activity for long. This is a recipe for monotony and boredom. If an activity ceases to be exciting, switch over to another one. This lowers your inertia and thus helps to avoid procrastination.

- Rest enough – REST! Your body. More so, your brain needs enough time to repair, rebuild and re-energize. Overworking your body and brain will create a natural resistance to a new undertaking. If this persists, it becomes habitual which eventually results in procrastination.

- Sleep well – sleeping is a deliberate part of resting. Yet, it is much more than normal resting. It is a state in which your body is subconsciously taken to a garage. When you fail to sleep enough, your brain becomes foggy. It fails to think fast on the next task to undertake. When it comes to sleep, focus on both quantity and quality. Have proper sleeping habits that ensure the quiet sleeping environment, respect to your circadian cycle and sufficient sleeping time.

- Plan always – planning, as we have seen, is a great way not to procrastinate. Many people procrastinate simply because there comes a time when nothing triggers them about the next task to do. Having a plan and using simple planning tools such as TO DO List, Diary, Journal, Alarm, etc, helps you to focus on implementing your plan.

Establish work boundaries

Clearly demarcate your work boundaries. Thoroughly comb through your Appointment letter and employment contract to understand your duties and responsibilities.

Avoid, without being prompted by your superiors, engaging in work that is outside your scope.

Other than work outside your scope, also, avoid engaging in relationships that are outside the scope of a structured formal work relationship.

Take clearly defined breaks such as tea break and lunch break seriously. Break off from work on time unless necessary.

Limit yourself to your officially designated workspace. Of course, you may be called to visit other workspaces and offices, but this should be in line with the execution of your duties and responsibilities. Simply do not trespass into other people's workspace.

Most importantly, do not engage in conversations that are out of the scope of work during working hours and in the workspace.

Establishing work boundaries will help you establish a mutually-beneficial professional working relationship with your juniors, peers, and superiors. It will also boost your productivity.

Chapter 13: How to Survive as an Empath

Empaths require survival tactics in order to flourish in an environment where they happen to be a minority.

When it comes to empaths, being susceptible to abuse and exploitation is more of a norm rather than an exception. This makes it extremely imperative that they learn to survive. While most empaths are highly intuitive, very few follow their intuition and thus end up doing contrary to what intuition warns them against... only to regret later.

More often than not, empaths ignore their intuition so as not to appear odd or simply to conform to insensitive societal demands and expectations. However, intuition is a defense mechanism and empaths must not sacrifice it for the sake of conformity or pleasing others. They have to rely on it.

They have to sharpen it. They have to make it their shield and defender.

The following are some of the ways by which empaths can survive in a world that neither understands them nor appreciates them... and at worst, find them human prey to ride on and bite.

Keep boundaries

Solitude is a natural way for empaths to keep boundaries. However, as social beings, they inevitably have to experience moments of interaction with other human beings. It is at such moments that keeping boundaries is important.

The following are some of the ways by which an empath can keep safe boundary:

- Stay focused – this is extremely important when it comes to conversations. It is no doubt that most empaths are introverts and as such, don't like being pushed to unnecessarily expose their inner feelings and thoughts. To avoid uncomfortable topics aimed at unduly exposing your privacy or secrets, stay focused on those topics you accepted to be involved in their discussion.

- Avoid temptations to overindulge – empaths like choosing wisely. They don't like doing things just to conform. They don't like being pushed to do that which they'd rather not do. Unfortunately, the world doesn't work that way, especially in social circles. Friends and peers are more likely to push one to overindulge in things that may not be positive such as bingeing, alcoholism, indecent exposure, among others. Due to being extremely self-aware, overly sensitive and more conscious, empaths suffer more from the consequences of such overindulgence than non-empaths. Thus, it is more honorable to disappoint and stay away from embarrassment than to please and end up being the one to carry the burden of disappointment.

- Protect your personal space – space intruders are many. There are those who do not respect personal space. To protect your personal space, you have to keep a safe distance of at least two feet from the closest person, if the person is not intimate.

- Avoid uncomfortable places – when you feel that certain places make you uncomfortable, simply keep off from them. There is an intuitive reason as to why you feel uncomfortable.

- Don't shy from walking away, if necessary – as a last resort, if you feel that, despite other efforts to protect your personal space and keep boundaries, someone or some people are not respectful, do not shy from walking away.

- Say NO! and keep it holy – practice to be assertive yet polite in saying NO! to indecent approaches and suggestions.

Keep off relationships that don't work

Empaths are more invested in relationships than non-empaths. Thus, it is hard for empaths to break relationships. However, relationships do come to an end – more often than not.

Clinging to relationships that no longer work or no longer inspire is one thing that empaths suffer from quite often. Empaths always harbor the hope that things can turn around and low ebbs are just seasonal.

When a relationship is persistently hurting despite your effort to turn it good; When your partner is no longer working towards it; When you are not appreciated by your partner despite being heavily invested in this relationship; it is time to let go. It is time to start disentangling yourself from it.

It can be such difficult, but not impossible. Slowly by slowly, gradually by gradually, a small step upon another, you will eventually overcome. What is important is to overcome your initial inertia and make a leap of faith. Don't doubt yourself nor blame yourself, that which comes alive will one time cease to be. A relationship is the same. There comes a time it comes to its end. This is the notion that we should embrace right at the beginning of relationships.

Detach yourself from the past

We are a product of the past. The past shaped our knowledge and continues to guide our steps in the present, and helps us visualize our future.

While the past is great, there are some hurtful elements of it that we must detach ourselves from. And while we cannot completely rid ourselves of the past for which we are made, we can detach ourselves from the experiences that are no longer worth it. Those experiences that hold us back and keep pricking our wounds.

For there to be healing, one must detach from the past hurtful experiences. There are times when a past experience was so good, so sweet, and so pleasant. For example a first date. Yet, a relationship that came from it is hurting, is not working, and has no better prospects.

Should one cling to that good past experience and use it as a justification to endure a toxic relationship? NO!

Just because someone did you a whole lot of great things in the past is not a justification for the person to persistently hurt and torment you.

Detect energy vampires

Vampires suck off your energy leaving you drained, fatigued, worn-out, dampened and at worst, depressed.

Vampires come in different shades and designs. Thus, to be able to deal with an energy vampire, first of all, you have to determine which type of vampire you are encountering.

The following are the six main types of energy vampires:

- Narcissistic vampire
- Victim vampire
- The dominator/controller vampire
- Melodramatic (histrionic) vampire
- Obsessive-compulsive vampire
- The judgmental (criticizer) vampire

- The bipolar (splitter) vampire

- Paranoic vampire

Narcissistic vampire

These are vampires who are extremely self-centered. They are incapable of empathy. They seek to use other people's energy for their own selfish gain. Since they have established their prowess as energy suckers, they are very quick at detecting empathetic prey... since empathetic preys are soft targets, easy to pierce through, and more enduring of the sucking pain.

Narcissistic vampires can be charming, pretentious and thus easily ensnare empaths into their energy-sucking dungeons.

Victim (martyr) vampire

These are vampires who prey on empaths' great sense of guilt. Victim vampires will tactically find channels to complain, blame, psychologically manipulate and emotionally blackmail empaths.

They are ever seeking validation, approval, and endless love from empaths. All these results in sucking so much energy from empaths.

The dominator/controller vampire

These are alpha vampires. They like feeling superior to others. To achieve this, they act to deflate the ego of those around them. They achieve this by piercing through other people's energy reserves and thus draining them off.

Naturally, dominator vampires are highly insecure and low-energy. So, for them to stay afloat, they have to inflate their energy from sucking others. And like narcissistic vampires, empaths become their easy prey.

Melodramatic (histrionic) vampire

Melodramatic vampires are attention seekers. Whatever you give your attention draws your energy. As such, melodramatic vampires are low-energy vampires that seek to boost their energy levels through attention-seeking.

To achieve their objectives, melodramatic vampires like creating a crisis. They exaggerate and magnify every little molehill into a giant mountain of problems.

And since empaths are active listeners, they easily get drained off by melodramatic vampires than non-empaths. It is quite easy for non-empaths just to ignore melodramatic vampires, which is not the case with empaths.

Obsessive-compulsive vampire

These come as perfectionists and workaholics. These are people who set impossible deadlines and threatening ultimatums. They like pushing people to the edge.

Most of the time, they are excellent performers. However, they don't appreciate other people's limitations. They want everyone to perform as they do. When others fail to perform as per their standards, they resort to punitive actions and aggressive behaviors.

Thus, they are autocratic in nature. They do not necessarily suck energy for themselves since they are already high-energy beasts. However, they drain your energy towards their goals. You are simply an expendable energy source for their mission.

You are like a donkey for their ride. They see you as nothing else but that. If you cannot expend sufficient energy, then, they see you as unworthy to them.

Empaths should guard against obsessive-compulsive vampires at workplaces. The workplace is where these vampires find a conducive environment to find their prey and exert their strangulating force.

The judgmental (criticizer) vampire

We all criticize at some point in time. Criticizing is not bad. It is what helps people to improve their thoughts and performance. However, excess of anything is poisonous. The same goes for criticizing.

There are those who are simply hypercritical. They are ever in a fault-finding mode. They simply look for an opportunity to find people's faults and amplify them.

They hardly offer any solution and neither are they themselves free from faults, but, they simply gain gratification from being hypercritical.

Judgmental vampires feed on other people's mental energy. They seek to control their thought process, invade their thoughts and channel the mental energy to their own thoughts.

Since empaths are highly sensitive, they become easy victims of judgmental vampires.

The bipolar (splitter) vampire

Have you met people whose moods change faster than the change in the weather? One moment they are radiating joy and the next moment they are radiating gloom? One moment they are laughing and the next moment they are quarreling? These are bipolar vampires.

Bipolar vampires are highly unpredictable. At one moment, they may seem the best of your friends, and at the next moment, they seem the worst of your enemies.

The energy flows in bipolar vampires is highly irregular. At one moment they are at their crest and at another moment they are at their trough. While we all go through mood swings, theirs is extremely of short wavelength such that these mood swings are more rapid and frequent than normal.

At their trough, the bipolar vampires require a lot of energy from the surroundings to rise up to the normal level. It is at the trough that they are the worst beasts, aggressive, angry, dangerous, suicidal, etc. They appear drowning and would want to cling on someone to remain afloat.

The sensitivity of empaths makes them highly susceptible to bipolar vampires. This is because empaths emotional energy oscillates with that of the people around them... and in the presence of bipolar vampires, the empaths are driven on a rollercoaster... lost and drained.

Paranoic vampire

Paranoic vampires are strikingly similar to the victim vampires. However, the main difference is the lack of self-pity on the part of paranoic vampires.

These vampires have a high level of distrust of those around them. They are ever suspicious of people. They do carry out rapid psychic scanning of those around them.

In this process of scanning, they drain other people's energy like a lab technician would suck your blood into a syringe for lab tests. Obviously, that blood is never returned back.

Paranoic vampires suck out empaths' energy for their own tests in a similar fashion. Due to their paranoia, they don't do this just once on a person, they do this repeatedly with a high level of frequency since their psychic scanner is easily triggered by any minute signal from the other person.

Paranoic vampires manifest themselves in their manner of extreme protest they make whenever they find you at fault. They will complain as to how you have seriously betrayed their trust and how they won't find it easy to trust you again.

Subconsciously, they are pushing you to allow them to suck out more energy from you towards their psychic lab test just to prove your level of trustworthy. And the vicious cycle continues.

Empaths suffer a lot more from paranoic vampires since they can't cope with highly suspicious persons. Empaths love being trusted and that's why most of them are honest. Piercing their trust using suspicious probes hurts them much more than it would hurt non-empaths.

How to handle energy vampires

Each type of vampire requires a unique kind of handling. However, there are general rules of thumb that cuts across.

The following are the general rules of thumb when it comes to handling any type of energy vampire:

- **Don't lose your self-esteem** – most energy vampires suffer from low self-esteem. Don't let their negative self-image about themselves become your self-image. What they paint of you is of their very own tainted lens. Don't see yourself from their tainted lens. Rather, see your self from your very own crystal –clear lens. To achieve this you need to cultivate a higher sense of self-awareness.

- **Boost your level of self-awareness** – to remain you, even in the extreme provocation, extreme criticism, blame games, etc, you've got to have a higher sense of self-awareness. Self-awareness enables you to look inwards and seek your true identity, true feelings, and true self-image rather than becoming prey to other people's identity of you, other people's feelings of you, and other people's image of you. To achieve a higher sense of self-awareness, you need to practice mindfulness meditation, reflection, and introspection.

- **Rise above them** – just as an eagle soars high to disable a ground prey, an empath has to soar high to disable energy vampires. When you remain grounded to their level, these bearish vampires will seize you and devour you. Rising high above their territory makes you more powerful and unreachable. How do you rise above? Rising above means being too high to be infected by their low self-esteem. It is about being too high for their energy-sucking proboscis to reach you. If it is criticism, rising high could including keeping off them and if you can't keep off them, disable them.

- **Cultivate a thick skin** – cultivating a thick skin means that you become impenetrable such that the vampires' energy-sucking proboscis cannot pierce through. Criticism, negative talks, gossips, insults, etc., cannot affect you. These are their piercing intrusions. When you develop a thick skin, instead of the vampires gaining more energy from you, they lose more in a failed attempt to suck from you and thus either die off or keep off.

- **Exercise your power** of NO! – one great weakness of most empaths is their inability to say NO! even when their powerful intuition tells them enough is enough. They still create a room, create more space for tolerance. They tolerate until they reach a level where the only coping mechanism is addiction and codependency.

How to deal with addiction

Empaths are more susceptible to addiction than non-empaths.

Addiction is a condition that makes a person engage in a behavior or consumption of a substance for the sake of gaining rewarding effects that have a highly compelling incentive for repetitive pursuit despite the adverse negative consequences.

While empaths may be less inclined to substance addiction than non-empaths, they are more inclined to certain 'positive' behavioral addiction than non-empaths.

Addiction triggers

Triggers play a critical role in enforcing addictive habits. Triggers lead to cravings and urge. A trigger is simply a cue that beckons a thought, feeling or action to consume an addictive substance or engage in addictive behavior.

There are two main types of triggers:

- Internal triggers
- External triggers

Internal triggers

These are triggers, which originate from within oneself. They can be thoughts, feelings or memories that become sensitized and hence bring forth urges and cravings.

There are three main types of internal triggers:

- Emotions
- Physical sensations

- Attitudes

Emotions

Emotions are by far the commonest of all addictive triggers. The following are some of the common emotions that can trigger one's addictive tendencies:

- Phobia
- Anxiety
- Loneliness
- Self-Pity
- Resentment
- Anger
- Indifference
- Boredom
- Fatigue

- Frustration
- Stress
- Depression
- Other negative feelings that one subconsciously endeavors to avoid

Phobia and anxiety

Phobia is an irrational and dilapidating fear characterized by extreme anxiety that severely interferes with quality of life or ability to function normally.

Phobia is characterized by two critical components:

- **Catastrophic thoughts** – thoughts about something bad happening
- **Evasive behavior** – taking action to avoid an occurrence of the perceived catastrophe

It is common to find people who have certain phobia resorting to drinking or taking marijuana in order to gain the confidence to deal with their phobias.

Some of the common phobias associated with addiction include:

- Social phobia (fear of public interactions) – this can make one seek substance abuse in order to feel comfortable in social places.

- Enochlophobia (fear of crowds) – this may aggravate emotional and social triggers.

- Glossophobia (fear of public speaking) – this may cause one to seek substance abuse in order to gain the confidence of addressing the public.

- Agliophobia (fear of pain)- this may trigger the abuse of opioids.

- Aviophobia (fear of flying) – this may aggravate emotional triggers.

- Monophobia (fear of being alone) – this may cause anger, resentment, self-pity, clinging, and obsession.

Physical sensations

Physical sensations can trigger addictive tendencies more so if they are associated with what you seek to remedy by consuming a given substance or engaging in certain addictive behavior.

The following are the common types of physical sensations:

- Pain
- Fatigue
- Panic
- Hunger
- Sexual arousal
- Senses (smells, tastes, sounds, touch, sight, etc)

External triggers

External triggers are those that originate outside oneself. The following are the two main types of external triggers:

- Environmental triggers
- Social triggers

Environmental triggers

Environmental triggers are those cues within your surroundings that bring about memories, feelings, and thoughts of addictive tendencies. The following are the two main types of environmental triggers:

- Places
- Things

Places

If you have a habit of engaging in addictive substance or behavior at a certain place, when visiting or being in that place will trigger the addictive tendencies.

The following are some of the high-risk places that can trigger addictive tendencies:

- Bars and clubs (alcohol and smoking)
- Hotels, restaurants and fast-food places (food addiction)
- Lodgings, Brothels and Massage parlors (sex addiction)
- Friend's home (cracking)
- Worksites (work addiction)
- Bathrooms (cracking, masturbation)
- Former drug-stash locations (cracking)
- Shopping malls (shopping addiction)
- Salons (cosmetic addiction)
- Gyms (exercise addiction)
- Casinos (gambling addiction)
- Cybercafés (digital addiction)

Things

There certain things that we often use while consuming addictive substances or carrying out addictive behaviors. Seeing these things will trigger addictive tendencies.

The following are high-risk things that can trigger addictive tendencies:

- Magazines (pornography addiction, sex addiction, food addiction, etc)
- Furniture (e.g. bed for sex addiction)
- Cash, Credit cards/ATMs – shopping addiction
- Empty pill bottles / unattended pills – drug addiction
- Television/movies - (pornography addiction, sex addiction, food addiction, etc)
- Wine/spirit bottle – alcohol addiction
- Bong – marijuana addiction

Situations

Situations and events can trigger addictive tendencies more so if one tends to engage in addictive activities during such situations/events.

The following are common situations/events that can trigger addictive tendencies:

- Emotionally charged interactions – e.g. upsetting news, political arguments, and criticism
- Holidays, celebrations, or sporting events – e.g. anniversaries, graduations, winnings
- Time-based events – e.g. breakfast (coffee), break time (junkie snacks), lunch and dinner time (bingeing), weekends (alcohol), Christmas season (bingeing, alcoholism), cold season (coffee)

How to deal with codependency

Codependency is a learned pattern of behaviors and beliefs that result in a relationship in which two people engage in mutually destructive habits and maladaptive coping mechanisms.

Maladaptive coping mechanisms are those mechanisms that a person adopts which limits the person's normal functioning and thus diminishes life satisfaction.

Parties to codependence

There are two parties to a codependent relationship:

- **The Taker**: The taker is that person in a relationship who seeks to be taken care of. The person is always looking to receive something from the relationship. As such, the taker exhibits almost opposite characters to the caretaker.

- **The Caretaker**: The caretaker is that person in a codependent relationship who seeks to nurture, to care, to offer help, to save and to see that the other person (taker) feels okay. More often than not, when people talk about codependence, their primary focus is on the caretaker. The taker is largely forgotten or overlooked.

How to break away from codependence

Breaking away from codependence is about learning, resetting your mindset and unwinding yourself from the entanglement of old habits that perpetuates codependence.

The following are the steps you need to take in order to break free from codependence:

- Look to Your Past
- Recognize Denial
- visualize your Ideal
- Detach and Disentangle Yourself
- Learn Independence
- Establish personal boundaries
- Create your own positive space
- Take breaks from each other
- Practice Self-care
- Learn to Say No!
- Learn to speak the truth
- Don't be a people-pleaser
- Focus on your preferences
- Don't be a slavish martyr
- Stop feeling personally responsible for others when you are not

- Resist the urge to offer unsolicited advice
- Think before committing to something
- Honor your needs
- Listen to your inner feelings
- When you are hurt, address the cause
- Do not insult your partner
- Find your way of handling a conflict
- Work on developing yourself
- Believe in yourself
- Keep a journal
- Lift your self-esteem and confidence
- Give without expecting anything in return
- Be around people who are good for you

Master the power of NO!

As we have seen above, being able to say NO! when your intuition tells so is what most empaths find it hard to do. Thus, they end up not sticking to their own demarcated boundaries and thus allow energy vampires not only into their personal space but also close enough to pierce their proboscis into them.

Mastering the power of NO! requires constant practice. It is about willpower. You have to raise your willpower to stand out and protect your boundaries. And just as a nation rises to protect its borders from intrusion, you have to be extra vigilant. You have to create a 'visa' to your territory and carefully assess the 'passports' of those who desire to enter your private domain. Those who don't meet the 'visa' criteria or have no 'passport' must not be allowed in. Yet, those who are allowed in and misbehave or proof ulterior motive, their 'visas' have been promptly canceled and confiscated so that at no other time should they be inadvertently be allowed in.

Yes, guard your personal space just as a nation guards its borders. Abide by your instinct. Set rules of evaluation of those you can allow close to you and those that you cannot. Set rules of engagement in all relationships and all activities and stick by them. Don't bend rules no matter the persuasions.

If you give in to persuasions, it becomes a dangerous habit that energy vampires turn into a chopping tool to your private domain. Keep safe by sealing off all potential fissures to your private space.

Chapter 14: How to Raise an Empath Child

Charity begins at home. And who an adult becomes is shaped by one's early childhood – at home. Thus, what an empath child turns out to be later on as an adult depends greatly on how that child is treated by parents at home and other caregivers.

An empath child is a normal child. Sometimes, parents who fail to understand and empath child might think that there is something odd with their child and thus take extra measures and actions that could be detrimental to the child.

The first thing a parent should do is identify a child's personality type. In identifying the personality type, the parent will establish whether the child is an empath or not.

How do you tell that your child is an empath?

There are many telling signs that your child is an empath. Nonetheless, the following are some of the most common telling signs:

1. **Extreme sensitivity to emotions around them**

   It is extreme sensitivity that makes most people label empath children as 'shy'. This is natural given that they absorb so many signals from a person such that they can easily have a clear picture of what a person is thinking about them and thus react – shyly.

2. **Easily overwhelmed by external stimuli**

   Empath children scan their environment like the way a revolving satellite dish does. Thus, they grab in a lot of signals from those around them and the environment.

This is why many of them are susceptible to allergic reactions. Certain perfumes, fabrics, or even colors can trigger an allergic reaction to them.

A lot of these are simply triggers of the image they stored in their mind when they encountered someone unpleasant. For example, an empath child will keep the memory of the scent, fabric texture and even color of the fabric of the person he/she responded negatively to. So, whenever the child encounters any of these triggers, there is an allergic reaction. This reaction can be physical, emotional, or psychosomatic.

3. **Bizarrely negative reaction to certain people or situations**

Empath children reach out beyond the outer appearance of the persons they encounter in their lives. They kind of dig deep into that person's soul.

And no matter how much the person disguises himself as a good person, the empath child will sense otherwise. Worse of it, the more the person pretends, the worse the negative reaction gets. This can cause the empath child, depending on age, to cry, to run away, to get angered, and even try to fight the person.

4. **Psychosomatically symptomatic**

Psychosomatic symptoms are those physical symptoms whose primary cause is not physiological but rather mental and/or emotional. Empath children manifest a high degree of psychosomatic symptoms that are related to the kind of emotions that they are experiencing.

Some of the psychosomatic symptoms include headaches, stomach upsets, allergy, sudden flu, among others. However, unlike physiological symptoms, psychosomatic symptoms easily disappear when their emotional stress is relieved. This relief can be in the form of a hug, the disappearance of an unwanted person from their vicinity, etc.

5. Transcendentally responsible

Empath children are transcendentally responsible. By transcendental, I mean that they overstretch their bounds of responsibility and thus instinctively take other people's responsibilities... not just physically but also psychospiritually.

Most empath children act like grown-ups when it comes to attending to other people's needs. They will try hard to make themselves available to serve those who are going through difficult situations, especially illness, financial troubles, among others. For example, when a parent is going through financial strain, the empath child will become frugal by skipping some meals, avoiding extravaganze, refusing to be pampered during birthday, etc.

6. Emotionally experience other people's pain

Empath children deeply experience the emotional pain of other people's suffering. Some, depending on their age, may cry when they see others cry, or they may try to help out to relieve their pain. This could including embracing those who are hurt, trying to provide a soothing item such as a hankie, a pillow, a teddy bear, some candy, beverage, etc. They may even refuse to go play or go to school just to be with a sick sibling or parent.

7. They get deeply hurt when wrongly reprimanded

Empath children have an extremely high sense of fairness and justice. Thus, when a parent scolds, reprimands or otherwise punishes them for mistakes not of their own making, they can take hours, days, or even months and years, just to get over it. This is unlike non-empath children who will easily shrug off and forget it in a short moment.

8. Feels comfortable playing alone

While a non-empath child feels uncomfortable playing alone, an empath child will easily feel comfortable playing alone. An empath child is deeply absorbed in the game, for example trying to explore the toy car, learn its mechanics and simply marvel at the car's movement. On the other hand, a non-empath child wants to play with others and kind of show off her new toy.

9. Takes a whole lot of time observing something

Empath children have a deeply keen sense of observation. They like being bystanders and just observe others act rather than being part of the game.

Their desire to observe rather than play a role can make them appear anti-social while they are not. Empath children hardly ask questions outwardly and hardly seek answers from others. But, they have more questions than non-empaths and sometimes feel that they will not even get answers from someone else. Thus, they like doing their own mental exploration through keen observation and find answers to their curiosity on their own.

10. They love personifying pets and objects

Empath children like personifying pets and objects. They will treat their pets just as they treat humans. They will also attach human meaning to their dolls. They will call names, embrace and adore their dolls just as they would do to human beings.

When someone mishandles or messes with their personified pets or objects, they feel emotionally hurt.

How to help an empath child deal with emotional issues

Once you detect that you have an empath child, the next important step is to learn how to handle the child. Many a time, parents make mistakes of trying to even out their children and so as to have a uniform blueprint of handling them. However, not all children are crafted from the same mold irrespective of them coming from the same womb.

Evening out children and smoothening off their differences kills their uniqueness. It dehorns a child's unique weapon of goring life's problems. The end result is having a docile, mediocre and unfulfilled adult.

Thus, it is important to learn how to handle each child based on that child's unique personality.

The following are some of the best ways to handle empath children:

1. **Teach them how to balance the power of solitude and the power of socialization**

   It is important to teach your empath child that desiring solitude is absolutely normal and healthy.

   Quite often, a lot of parents discourage their empath children from solitude by associating solitude with weirdness, wickedness, and such other negative connotations. This makes empath children become guilty of their very own nature.

   Instead, teach your empath child the virtues of solitude. Yet, without discouraging solitude, teach your child the virtues of socialization without seemingly biased in favor of socialization.

Let the child learn that both worlds are important. Both worlds are like a pair of binoculars that makes the vision clearer.

2. Teach them meditation

More often than not, many parents assume meditation is only for adults. They do not fathom the possibility that children can also practice meditation.

While empath children are naturally predisposed to meditation, and which they often do, sometimes they do not recognize that they are doing it. A lot of times, they may try to obscure or even obfuscate their moment of meditation when they realize that someone is being drawn to their act of meditating.

Thus, unlike non-empaths, it is quite easy to teach empaths how to meditate by simply making them aware of what they already do and emphasizing its importance and the various techniques of doing it.

More important than anything else, child empaths need assurance from their parents that engaging in meditation is not abnormal. It is perfectly normal. This way, empath children won't have a negative association with meditation and won't feel guilty of being blank and staring. Make them know that it is absolutely normal and necessary.

3. Teach them how to practice the art of freeing up the flow of emotional energy

Emotional overload is what most empath children suffer from almost all the active time. As such, it is important to help your empath children unload overwhelming emotions. It is important to teach them emotions are bundles of energy and they just accumulate as water does in a dam. If there is no exit during flooding, the dam's walls may break due to excessive pressure. The same is the case with emotional energy.

Teach your empath child the art of freeing up the flow of emotional energy. Physical activities such as yoga, swimming, and choreographic dance are extremely helpful in not only relieving off emotional overload but also unclogging channels of energy flow so that emotional energy does not accumulate to dangerous levels.

Apart from the mentioned physical exercises, creative art such as drawing, doodling, molding objects, and writing – especially poetry, can be great channels through which bloated emotional energy can be deflated.

4. Teach them how to avoid becoming preys to energy vampires

Empaths have characteristic attributes that make them appear as instant preys to energy vampires. Being children makes such empaths even more vulnerable.

One important way to help empath children avoid becoming easily susceptible prey to energy vampires is to train them to rely on their already powerful intuition. More often than not, empaths detect danger, but, just as you mute an alarm when the sleep is too sweet to wake up, empaths can mute their intuition just to fit into situations.

One important aspect of this intuition training is to teach your empath child the power of NO! Let the child be able to say no whenever he/she feels vulnerable or likely to be exploited, especially by sexual pests who may use emotional manipulation to their advantage.

5. Teach them the benefits of their unique nature and how they can explore them

Empaths have a unique nature, and with it comes a whole package of goodies to offer the world. While we may not tell what goodies rest hidden in each empath's pack, it is important to encourage them to unleash the goodies.

There are great fetes that have been achieved by empaths that ordinarily appeared impossible to achieve. And if humanity has to extend the bounds of possibilities, then, empaths have to be encouraged by providing them with space, and opportunity for them to unleash their hidden potential.

How to help an empath child deal with relationship issues

Empath children can have a difficult relationship with others, more so with superiors. They may appear as indisciplined, needy, overly sensitive, 'big-eyed/jealous' (because they demand fairness), and difficult to manage (because they are not easily flattered).

In this case, it is important to provide counseling and conflict management. It is important to make the child understand the superiors just as it is important to make superiors understand the child. This will help to limit perceptional problems that breed conflict.

How to help an empath child deal with energy issues

The best way to help an empath child deal with energy issues is to learn the child. Learn potential triggers that can result in energy dissipation from the child. Encourage the child to confide in you and learn to be highly confidential and trustworthy.

Empaths tend to believe that a secret is the only asset they truly own in this world. As such, if you don't treat the information they provide to you with strict confidentiality, they are bound to lose trust in you. When that trust is lost, it is the hardest one to repair.

The child can be helped to deal with energy issues just as an adult empath. Only that you have to be ready to walk together with the child as the child navigates this journey. Confidence and support are what the child needs to be assured of making the right steps.

How to help an empath child achieve the highest level of creative aspirations

Every child has something unique to offer to the world, empath children are not an exception. They too have something unique to offer to the world. What might be a bit challenging is to uncover that which is hidden within them since most of the empaths are introverted.

Take an empath child like a human lab. Explore the child. Experiment with various activities and undertakings just to learn what might interest the child and trigger the hidden talent. Invest a lot in exploration and experimentation. It is such an investment that will last a lifetime – and it could change the world.

PART IV: HOW TO MAINTAIN YOUR WELLBEING WHEN LIFE HURTS

Overview

It is commonly said that empaths think with their emotions. The biggest challenge of relying on emotions to make decisions and take actions is that emotions are highly volatile.

Worst of it, empaths experience higher levels of emotional volatility than non-empaths. And thus, become victims of the turmoils of their very own emotions.

Life at times hurts, and hurts empaths much more than non-empaths, given the same circumstances. This is mainly because empaths invest so much in trust and faith in other people. As such, when such trust and faith is betrayed, it leaves deep wounds – and scars if healed.

It thus becomes imperative for Empaths to focus deeply on their wellbeing to protect it from vagaries of emotional turbulence and betrayal of trust – a betrayal that is almost a norm rather than an exception in the increasingly competitive world marked by survival for the fittest.

In this battle of survival for the fittest, narcissistic energy vampires are ever ready to prey on empaths as their ready meal.

It is hard to completely avoid bites from these vampires, thus, empaths have a greater responsibility towards treating their wounds and tending to their scars in such a way that doesn't permanently disorient them from their nature of being.

In this Part, we are going to focus on how empaths can maintain their wellbeing when life inevitably hurts.

Step One: Make a bold decision

Life is not lost by dying; life is lost minute by minute, day by dragging day, in all the thousand small uncaring ways.

--- Stephen Vincent Benét ---

Life is about choices. Every moment there is a choice to make – to wake up or not, to breath or not, to eat or not, to go to work or not, to go to school or not, among so many others. Forget about the common misstatement "I have no choice"! There is no situation where you have no choice. Every situation has a choice. Maybe the options may not be such appealing or desired, but, there is a choice nonetheless. Without choices, there is no life. Yet, every choice has a consequence.

Certain key ingredients characterize a choice;

- Intent
- Timeframe
- Effort

Intent

There is no choice without an intent/purpose. What is your intent in making a certain choice? That determines the value that you have decided to assign your choice. For example, you can choose to snap out of endlessly mourning your loved one or you can choose to steep yourself into the depth of mourning, continuing to dig more and more every passing day till your life ceases to be. Conversely, you can choose to decide that bygones are bygones. You have no control over what happened. You cannot change the past and hence decide to snap out, recollect yourself and be ready to confront the future and you become self-aware of the present that the moment of now has gifted you. Thus, your intent determines the extent to which your life hurts.

Timeframe

Every choice must be made within a certain timeframe, not just time. Time is limitless. It is only a 'frame' of it that you have cut out that is limited. For a decision to be termed as a decision, it must have a time frame within which it has to be implemented. For example, when do you decide to get over with divorce? To get over with the death of a loved one? You can choose to procrastinate as you wait for the event to miraculously happen by itself or you can make a bold decision to get over it right now, in this very present moment! Life continues to hurt the moment you surrender your bad situation to procrastination.

Effort

An effort is an energy in action that is driven towards the achievement of a certain specific intent. The energy that is not driven towards a certain specific intent is not effort but wasted energy. Whenever there is an effort, it is always driven towards countering force – inertia. It is only after there is enough force to overcome the inertia that things start moving from potential to kinetic (energy in action). Yes, your world starts moving the moment you overcome your inertia (procrastination, dwelling in the past, exploring your pain, etc). The same applies to hurt. Life hurts for so long as you don't put effort to push it away from a hurting situation.

So, what is a bold decision?

A bold decision is one where the various elements of its choice are fully optimized. Yes, it is optimized when the intent is the most supreme of them all (with the highest possible opportunity cost); the timeframe is of utmost priority and the effort is fully dedicated.

Our modern lifestyles have brought us the misconception that big is better. Thus, we focus on grandiose schemes of things to the detriment of small details that would actually add more value to our lifestyles and bring forth the grandest of our being.

It's the little decisions we make every day that will either bring us closer to our goals or further away from them. Be mindful of the choices you are making when going through a difficult time. For example: If your goal is to move through the pain of life and get out the other side with your head held high, then, your choices will come down to as simple things as: going for a walk, taking up a new hobby, accepting friends requests to catch up, going to bed early and getting sleep, make the decision to not to inadvertently assign time to your trauma however pricking it is. This is the best way to snap out of it. It all starts with a very minor decision such as making a call to a colleague; visiting a loved one; deciding to play with and entertain a neighbour's kid; taking a dog for a walk; deciding to teach some kids a music or art lesson; deciding to enrol with a charity, community mobilization, or relief organization, etc. Opportunities are all over for you to start small and grow big. So, don't think there is such a big decision that you must make to get out of a hurting situation. Very small bold decisions can have a giant effect just like a persistent small ax felling a giant tree.

"Big, sweeping life changes really boil down to small, everyday decisions"

--- Ali Vincent ---

It is in the small decisions you and I make every day that create our destiny

---Tony Robbins ---

What would happen if you make that small decision that every morning, no matter your schedule of work or study, you must have sufficient sunshine exposure? What would happen when you make that small decision that every day you must clear some dirt and educate those close to you to ensure a clean environment just to have fresh breath? What would happen if you make a small decision that better a small house surrounded by a natural environment than a grand house in a concrete jungle? What would happen if you make that small decision that instead of smoking tobacco or buying products from water and air-polluting factories you would rather enjoy some wild fruits and vegetables? The world would start getting transformed! You are the world without whom it can't simply exist! Your decision, no matter how small it is, for so long as it is for the greater good, is a world-changing transformation. When life hurts, don't go on with the hurting path. Seek that which makes life better. It doesn't have to be directly related to that which is hurting you, but eventually, it will come to be a healing remedy to your hurt. Nature is wholesome. Whatever little thing you do to make it better blesses you in unexpected ways.

What is the first and foremost bold decision should you make?

Understanding your mind!

Understanding your mind is not only the first and foremost bold decision to make but also a journey into self-discovery. It is a journey akin to that of a diver going undersea to discover the new world beneath or of an astronaut endeavoring to discover the marvelous heavens in the space beyond the earth. It is a new paradigm shift in the way of discovery.

Yet, unlike discovering the treasure hidden within the ocean or the new heavens beyond the space, understanding your mind is a journey that is within you. It is a journey that you always make an effort and travel towards it. But, since curiosity has never met you to ask you what rests beyond your conscious horizon, you've never attempted to go beyond the conscious village that is within your mind. And probably, you have never attempted to scratch beyond the surface to discover the hidden treasures below where you stand. Have you?

Fortunately, this book is that probing curiosity. It is seeking to prompt you to the exposure of nakedness of knowledge. A knowledge that is hardly new, but, probably had been a secret kept from you for ages by the veil of your very own unconsciousness. Yes, knowledge of the world within you. You have to unlock this knowledge.

It is commonly said that experience is not what happened to you but how you respond to that which happened to you. This response will determine whether you will lead a hurting life or not. Yet, this response is a product of your very own mind. The key to unlocking yourself from a hurting life rests deep in your mind.

Discover the key!

Step Two: Take control of your situation

*God, give me the grace to accept with serenity
the things that cannot be changed,
Courage to change the things
which should be changed,
and the Wisdom to distinguish
the one from the other.*

--- *Reinhold Niebuhr (1892-1971)* ---

There are things within our control and there are things that we have no control over such as the weather. People with mental health issues will often spend much time and energy on things that they have no control over. Be mindful of the amount of time you are spending thinking about things that you cannot change or are unhelpful to you. For example, if you are feeling angry or sad about things that have happened to you in the past this is not something that you can change. The past is in the past and you cannot change this. Energy spent dwelling on this past is wasted energy.

Do not let what is out of your control interfere with all the things you can control

As put forth by Reinhold Niebuhr, there are those things that you can change and there are those that cannot be changed. It is important to know the difference!

Many times, we spend a bigger part of our lives trying to move huge mountains when probably what we required was simply to acknowledge and admire their uniqueness. We only needed to take a step to climb them, see what is hidden beyond them and appreciate the panoramic view of that newness that we soon needed to discover.

The fallacy of many of us is to imagine that we can endeavor to use all our might to change the world. This is ably captured by the following famous quote;

> *When I was a young man, I wanted to change the world. I found it was difficult to change the world, so I tried to change my nation. When I found I couldn't change the nation, I began to focus on my town. I couldn't change the town and as an older man, I tried to change my family. Now, as a bedridden sick old man, I realize the only thing I can change is myself, and suddenly I realize that if long ago I had changed myself, I could have made an impact on my family. My family and I could have made an impact on our town. Their impact could have changed the nation and I could indeed have changed the world.*
>
> ***- Author Unknown -***

You are the world without which it cannot exist. Change yourself and you will indeed change the world. It all begins with your mindset. Check your bio-software. Iterate through it. Test it, debug it and retest it. If it is working perfectly, in harmony and aligned with your highest aspirations, you will achieve that which can only be imagined by others as miracles.

The greatest determinant of what you can change and what you cannot change is your willpower. This willpower is fuelled by a very powerful propellant – your ATTITUDE. Your attitude determines your willpower. Yet, your attitude and willpower are both products of your very own mindset!

What are the things that you cannot change?

You cannot change;

- **Your past** – your past happened and it cannot be changed. What matters are the lessons that you learned. Don't attach yourself to the past occurrences but derive pure lessons for future applications.

- **Your future** – your future is not yet born. You are not certain that you will live it. Thus, it is good to plan for it, but, don't let it sweep away your joys of the moment. Don't let it take away more than a fair share of what it deserves.

- **People's perception of you** – for so long as you are not alone, there will always be people's perception of you. There is nothing you can do to change people's perceptions but there is everything you can do to change yourself.

What are the things that you can change?

- **Your attitude** – your attitude drives you. It is the ignition key to your willpower.

- **Your willpower** – your willpower is kinetic energy which propels you to take appropriate action to change. Make sure that you are full of it.

- **Your self-image** – your self-image is a reflection of who you think you are. Sometimes your self-image can be true or false. You need a true self-image in order to discover your true being, purpose, and aspirations.

Step Three: Take charge of your emotions

Other than the physical hurt, emotional hurt is one of the most commonly talked about of life hurts. In fact, more people encounter emotional hurts than physical hurts. The most enduring elements of a hurting life are rarely physical but emotional.

It is quite obvious that everyone has experienced emotions in one way or another to varying degrees. Just like love, emotion is one of those areas that, although their experience is easy to tell, there is no exact universally agreed definition.

To be able to take charge of your emotions, the most fundamental step is to understand what they are, what their purpose is, how they come about and how you can intelligently apply them to fit different situations.

What is an emotion?

One of the best definitions or perspectives of emotion is one put forth by Hockenbury who defines emotion as "a complex psychological state that involves three distinct components; a subjective experience, a physiological response, and a behavioral or expressive response."

Subjective experience (how we experience the emotion): Experiencing emotions is highly subjective and depends on one's background, culture or environment. However, the following are common subjective labels; 'angry', 'sad', 'annoyed', 'joyful', 'happy', etc. These are relatively universal though their intensity varies from person to person.

Physiological response (how our body reacts to the emotion): heart palpation from fear and stomach lurches from anxiety are some of the physiological reactions. Sweating palms, heartbeats and rapid breathing are some of the common physical responses that occur during an emotional encounter.

Behavioral response (how we behave in response to the emotion): this is the action part – the actual expression of emotion. Common expressions include smile to indicate pleasure, happiness, joy or satisfaction; a frown to indicate displeasure or sadness. Emotional intelligence enables one to appropriately interpret these behavioral responses.

Why do you need emotions?

Emotions, though at times can work to our detriment, that's not the purpose of them. Emotion plays an important role in our wellbeing;

Emotions can motivate us to act positively: anxiety about certain things, for example, an exam, can cause us to take action to prevent undesired results. Fear of exam failure can motivate us to study more and harder in order to pass. On the other hand, not wanting to experience negative emotion such as anger and sadness can motivate us to take up activities that enhance our happiness and satisfaction such as social activities (meeting friends, participating in charity work, etc) and hobbies (such as swimming, listening to music, dancing, sports, etc).

Emotions can help us survive, avoid danger and thrive: Emotions are an adaptive mechanism that helps us maximize our chances of survival and success by motivating us to take quick actions that result into either fight (confront the source of our irritation when we are angry) or flight (run away from impending danger when we are fearful). Other than fight or flight, emotion such as love can help us seek out mates and reproduce thus enhancing the survival of human species.

Emotions boost our decision-making ability: Studies have ascertained that people who, due to certain brain damage, are unable to experience emotion have decreased capacity to make good decisions. Thus, emotions greatly influence the decisions that we make; be it spending money, eating, exercising, voting, mating, and marrying, among other decisions. This is why emotional intelligence is part and parcel of every decision that we make, whether they are deemed rational or logical or not.

Emotions enable us to understand other people: emotional expressions are a very powerful form of communication. We know how important communication is in social relationships. Thus, emotions help us understand others' responses to our expression. This makes us become more aware of them and better understand them. Positive emotional expressions such as expression of love and appreciation affirm our conduct and thus helps us deepen our relationships. Negative emotional expressions such as anger and displeasure help us realize that our conduct is probably not conducive to our relationships and thus helps us make appropriate adjustments.

Emotions enable other people to understand us: as a form of communication, our emotional expressions give feedback to other people about their words and deeds. This enables them to understand our preferences, likes and dislikes thus enhancing our mutual relationships.

How do emotions come about?

Emotions are created or triggered in the brain. Thus, they are a function of the brain. Hence, that which affects or influences the brain has the ability to affect or influence our emotions. This is very important as it helps us understand that we can develop and enhance our emotional intelligence by working on our brain neuro-circuitry – and, of course, our mindset.

Emotional intelligence

Emotional intelligence refers to the capability of human beings to recognize their own and other people's emotions, to differentiate between different feelings and tag them appropriately, to apply emotions in guiding thinking and behavior, and to manage or alter them so as to achieve one's goals or adapt to the existing environment.

According to Daniel Goleman, an expert in emotional intelligence, there are five core competencies of emotional intelligence;

1. **Self-awareness** – This is the ability to know oneself including one's emotions, weaknesses, strengths, goals, core values, drive, and recognizing their impact on others and making appropriate decisions to achieve desired intent.

2. Self-regulation – This is being in control of one's disruptive emotions and impulses and redirecting them to adapt to changing circumstances.

3. Social skill – this is a skill set that enables one to manage relationships and lead people to the desired direction in order to achieve the desired outcome.

4. Empathy – this is the ability to put into consideration other people's feelings and factoring them as part of the decision-making process.

5. Motivation – this is the ability to drive oneself towards the achievement of certain objectives

How to boost one's emotional intelligence

The five key competencies inform us of the key areas that we have to improve on in order to boost our emotional intelligence. Ensuring that each of these key competencies is optimized is the best way to boost one's emotional intelligence.

The following are some of the ways to boost each of these core competencies;

Boosting self-awareness: You can boost self-awareness through mindfulness meditation.

Enhancing self-regulation: Self-regulation is about the power to take charge of your emotions. This so much to do with your willpower, so, you have to increase your willpower.

Building stronger social skills: stronger social skills can be built by engaging the right association (see Step 5) through social activities and team-building efforts.

Deepening empathy: The best way to deepen one's empathy is by practicing compassion; both self-compassion and compassion towards others (see Step 7).

Increasing one's motivation: motivation can be enhanced by challenging yourself to make bold decisions (see Step 1), taking control of your situation (see Step 2) and being focused (see Step 4).

Willpower as the primary agent of self-regulation and control

> *Willpower isn't just a skill. It's a muscle, like the muscles in your arms or legs, and it gets tired as it works harder, so there's less power left over for other things*
>
> --- **Charles Duhigg** ---

What is willpower?

Willpower is the most omnipotent word when it comes to changing your mindset and thus overcoming your trauma. It is the orbit that other methods and strategies revolve around and without which the center cannot hold. Willpower is a compound word that blends two important words 'will' and 'power'. Thus, to comprehensively understand it, it is important to first digest what will is before digesting what willpower is.

Will is the ability to make a conscious choice. We all have free will and make our own choices, even if these are to obey the commands of others. A person may be described as 'wilful' (as opposed to 'willingful') if they do not easily submit to the requests or commands of others.

Willpower is the motivation to exercise will. A person with strong willpower will assert decisions even in the face of strong opposition or other contradictory indicators. A person with little willpower will give in easily (become complacent).

Getting what you want takes willpower, whether it means you doing something or others doing things for you. To succeed, this means you must first know what you want. Then you must be determined to get it, even in the face of extreme difficulties.

Will and power are closely related, as using will is, in essence, exercising power. Powerful people often exercise what seems to be a strong will, although this often comes from the confidence that having power creates rather than directly from having the power. In a reversal, people who have strong will increase their power as a result.

What breeds willpower?

Willpower is the product of the ingenious programming of your mindset such that the input that gets into your mind gets an output that propels you into positive action. This positive action is excited by the positive self-image that you manifest from the feedback of the processing function within your brain. It is like typing something onto the keyboard and what you get on the screen makes you laugh, exclaim and ooze confidence that you are ready to pursue your goals. Sometimes, you may type the same thing, and depending on the mindset (how the mind is programmed or 'set') you get onto the screen some image or content that dampens your spirit forces you to switch off the computer and wallow in the misery of negative thoughts. The difference between the two experiences is how you programmed your mindset.

The importance of emotional intelligence and willpower in healing a hurting life

Both emotional intelligence and willpower are a function of the mind. We've seen how the most enduring element of a hurting life is emotions. A lot of times, we are emotionally hurt not because of the deliberate intents of our loved ones but from our misinterpretation and misunderstanding of their emotional expressions and behaviors. Indeed, the biggest and most significant portion of our emotional hurts is due to our very own misinterpretations and misunderstandings.

Emotional intelligence helps us avoid these misinterpretations and misunderstandings thus significantly cutting down on the sources of our lives' hurts. With emotional intelligence, we can lessen the incidences and mitigate the damages of a hurting life.

With willpower, we can be able to make bold informed decisions about what we have gathered through our emotional intelligence. It could be a bold decision to walk out of a relationship that no longer serves your highest aspirations. It could be a bold decision to accept that your loved one has moved on and it is no longer tenable to keep following him/her expecting them to change their minds thus getting more hurt in the process.

Yes, with great emotional intelligence accompanied by strong willpower, you can easily take charge of your emotions and go a long way in healing a hurting life.

Step Four: Be Focused

Living one day at a time,

Enjoying one moment at a time,

Accepting hardship as a pathway to peace,

Taking, as Jesus did,

This sinful world as it is,

Not as I would have it,

Trusting that You will make all things right,

If I surrender to Your will,

So that I may be reasonably happy in this life,

And supremely happy with You forever in the next.

Amen.

--- Reinhold Niebuhr (1892-1971) ---

Focusing is a mental phenomenon. When you are mentally disturbed, such as when you are filled with worries, anxiety, stress and even depression, there are plenty of thoughts razing through your mind such that you cannot focus on a certain specific thought that is of importance to your present needs.

Thus, the best way to be focused is to de-clutter your mind from these razing thoughts. A free mind is a focused mind. Yet, for this mind to be free, it must not be tethered to the past nor catapulted to the future. It must be free to the present unwrapping in the moment of now.

All that we are is the result of what we have thought. The mind is everything. What we think we become.

--- Buddha

Your mind is run by the mindset. A defective mindset is like a computer that has been infected by a virus – many unwanted programs are running through uncontrollably. Sometimes you may see strange codes on the screen, weird messages flowing through, the CPU overheating (just like your head getting hot and aching), memory getting full thus resulting in dragging of execution of instructions. This is the very same kind of thing that runs through your mind when a defective mindset is allowed to work.

A people with an infected mindset can see weird images or ghosts, become terrified, scream, fear darkness, lose sleep, etc. They become seized with hallucinations, hysteria, and phobia, among other mental illnesses. These are akin to experiences in hell – of a hurting life.

What should you do? The first and foremost thing to do is to change your mindset (just like removing/cleaning/debugging the infected software). Once you change your mindset, then you can start engaging other remedial actions such as feeding in the right input (thoughts), etc.

Your thought depends on;

- The mental image you stored in your memory
- The meta tag that references to your mental image
- How you programmed your mind to respond to the incoming signal that is referenced by the meta tag

Change your mindset

Your mindset refers to how you programmed your mind to respond to a certain signal (stimuli). Different people would have different thoughts of the same signals and consequently different responses. This difference is not caused by the signal but by the mental image you've stored in your mind and your mindset (how you've programmed your response to that which resembles the stored mental image).

Everything that you store in your memory is stored in the form of a mental image. This image has special meta tags that describe that which is stored as uniquely identifiable from the rest and which can easily be searched and sorted by your brain.

You cannot force yourself to forget. But, you can change the meta tag to a mental image of that which is stored. For example, one person can have a mental image of the waterfall with a meta tag as 'drowning!' while another one may have it with a meta tag as 'swimming!' each of these two meta tags represents the past experience of what one encountered with waterfall. The one who drowned will have the 'drowning!' meta tag while the one who swam will have the 'swimming!' meta tag. Each of these meta tags will have a program (mindset) associated with the appropriate response. The 'drowning!' meta tag will generate a negative kind of response such as 'run-away!' while the 'swimming!' meta tag will have a positive kind of response such as 'get clothes off and swim!'.

While you cannot change the 'waterfall' image in your memory, you can change the 'drowning!' meta tag and in effect change the 'run-away!' mindset. This, in essence, is changing your life from a hurting life to a joyful life.

The waterfall experience is such an obvious experience. However, we do have certain other experiences that happened to us when we were not aware (maybe happened when we were babies) and which we programmed our minds to respond to them in a certain way. It is a bit difficult to change their meta tags since we can't exactly remember them. If we can't change their meta tags, then it becomes so hard to change the program (mindset) since this mindset has the meta tag referenced to it. However difficult it is, it is not impossible! Through the power of meditation, it is possible to get into the depth of the thoughts and be able to unearth the meta tags and change them. The good thing is that, since we were not aware of the occurrence, once we alter the meta tag, then it becomes easy to alter the mindset.

What do you need in order to change your mindset?

In the previous step, we saw how your attitude determines your willpower. An attitude is a learned predisposition to think, feel or act in a certain way. Just as you learn it, you too can unlearn it.

What triggers this unlearning? Unlearning is triggered by self-awareness. Self-awareness is having a clear insight into your personality. This personality includes your thoughts, feelings, strengths, weaknesses, attitudes, beliefs and motivations, among others.

When you become self-aware, you realize your purpose in life, what you need to do in order to achieve it and what hinders you from achieving it.

What triggers the change? Once you become self-aware, you cannot change unless you have;

- Will – will refer to the desire to do take some action.
- Power – power refers to the capacity and ability to execute your will.

Yes, it is a willpower that triggers your change action.

Make your self-aware

Not all people are capable of being self-aware. Even those who are self-aware, they probably have not optimized this self-awareness.

The following are some of the approaches you can embrace to become self-aware and optimize it;

- Psychometric tests – there are plenty of psychometric tests designed to help you do self-diagnosis so that you become more aware of yourself.

- Exploration – exploration is about setting yourself up to new experiences and gauging how you perform. In this performance, you can discover your strengths, weaknesses, opportunities, and threats.

- Storytelling – the best story you can ever tell someone is yourself. In telling your trusted friends and loving members about yourself, you expose yourself to being evaluated and being informed about your attitude, your strengths, weaknesses, and much more important, what you need to do in order to be a better you.

- Writing – writing is extremely powerful. I have experienced the power of writing. It is one of the most important therapies you can carry on yourself. The most difficult kind of writing that people avoid is about their feelings and emotions. Yet, in feelings and emotions rests the most powerful force of energy that you can ever possess.

- Role-making – decide the role that fits you well. Learn it. Master it and become its specialist.

- Coaching – there are many life coaches out there waiting to help you out. Even if the other methods highlighted above works for you, a professional touch too does help.

Don't ask yourself what the world needs; ask yourself what makes you come alive. And then go and do that. Because what the world needs are people who have come alive.

--- Harold Whitman ---

Change your self-image

Amongst the most important mental images you have is your self-image. Your self-image is built based on the following;

- Your experiences. As said earlier, your experience is less about what happened to you but more about what you did with what happened to you. In experience, your response matters most. If you live regretting your past response then, this will impact negatively on your self-image where you feel less-than-perfect, weak, incapable, undeserving, among others – thus, making you lead a hurting life. However, if you live celebrating your past response, then, this will impart a positive self-image. You will feel powerful, confident, assertive, strong, perfect and ready to face more challenges – hence, living a happy life.
- What you perceive about you. Your perceptions too influence your self-image. The greatest source of your perception is from what you perceive about yourself from others' responses

to your interaction with them. If you sense frequent or constant rejection in your interaction with others, you are more likely going to have a negative self-image of a social misfit. Thus, you will perceive life hurts. However, if you sense frequent or constant acceptance from your interaction with others, then you are going to have a positive self-image of someone worthy, someone wanted, someone loved and someone respected. Hence you will perceive life joys.

You are not defined by your experiences and perceptions but who you truly are. Through self-awareness, you can get rid of the false image, be it negative or positively exaggerated.

Regain your willpower: put your power and your will into action

In the previous step, we discussed what willpower is and that which makes it get depleted.

Sometimes your willpower gets worn out by carrying excessive baggage that you don't need to – Yesterday and Tomorrow – such that your willpower muscle gets worn out. Don't allow these two pieces of baggage to be heavier than the muscles you have in the present moment of today.

As Reinhold Niebuhr advises, live one day at a time. Enjoy one moment at a time. This is the way you were meant to live. Be the present that you desire today.

There are times hardships come by. Learning from masters of extreme fitness, these hardships help to strengthen your resolve and make your load lighter. Don't evade them, don't avoid them. But, do confront them with wisdom and acuity. Just do that which you ought to do in the moment of now and everything else will fall in line.

As Charles Duhigg puts it, your willpower can get depleted just as your energy during fitness workouts. However, there is nothing as bad to your body as a lack of fitness workouts. The same applies to your willpower.

Your willpower is enhanced by taking more and greater challenges. But, take them in such a manner that you don't become chronically depleted.

What you focus on grows, what you think about expands, and what you dwell upon determines your destiny.

--- Robin Sharma ---

Do start now!

Procrastination is the thief of will, power and time. The five most important things that you must start doing now in order to become self-aware, strengthen your willpower and change your mindset are;

1. Discover who you are

2. Set out goals to achieve your life purpose

3. Identify your negative attitude, your negative self-image, and every other hindrance that you perceive as preventing you from achieving your goal

4. Plan to change your mindset by identifying the required positive attitude, your required positive self-image all other things that you think are going to work towards overcoming your hindrances. Set milestones that you ought to achieve in executing your plan starting from the present moment.

5. Execute your plan now!

Step Five: Engage the right association

I am because you are

--- The spirit of Ubuntu ---

We, humans, are social beings. Without social interactions, the worth of a human being declines to zero. This is why most lonely people raze with suicidal thoughts in their minds while some actual commit to these thoughts. Without others, you cannot be.

Thus, to be a better you, to become all you need to be, you must engage the right association. The greatness of a person is the association that he keeps. This is evidently true in business, in the profession, in politics, and in all faculties of life.

Thus, to engage the right association is to experience life joys. To engage the wrong association is to experience life hurts. The choice is yours! Make yourself happy.

Tell me your friends and I will tell who you are

There is that kind of natural repulsion that happens when you try to engage in friendship with a person who can't be. Becoming someone's friend is such a subtle natural selection that depends so much on your inner being.

It depends so much on your emotional intelligence than anything else. It is more of a gut feeling. When you try to force a friendship that doesn't or ought not to exist, life will inevitably hurt.

When you allow yourself to experience the spontaneity of friendship as it arises, you will experience a happy, joyful life.

You are the company that you keep

Yet, friends are not just for interaction. Friends shape you and in the process you shape them. You become one in so many aspects. That's why it is easy to know and understand someone by studying the company that he/she keeps. Hence, if you want to be judged well, then, keep the right associations! To become a better you, a joyful you, a happy you, keep the right company and surely life won't hurt.

The association promotes a way of life, not causes; a harmony in living, not political faiths; a bilateral loyalty, not commercial or social projects. Yet it is an association for as noble a purpose as any involved in any prior decisions.

--- William O. Douglas ---

Your associations become your lifestyle. Without associations, there is no lifestyle! Thus, if there is a certain kind of lifestyle that you admire or aspire to have, seek association with people who are already living it. Work towards it. This is the ultimate wealth that you can ever acquire. All other forms of wealth will ultimately fall in line.

You do not attain success when you associate with those in high positions. It comes when you accept yourself and realize that only you can take yourself to where your heart truly lies.

--- Michael Bassey Johnson ---

You cannot forge your associations just as you cannot forge your friendship. This can only come from your inner desire. This must be cultivated by the efforts of your emotional intelligence. Your associations are like climbing stairs. Having stairs does not guarantee you to the top; they only provide the ways and means. It is up to you to take the action of climbing on the stairs to the top. It is up to you to marshal your sinews to continue climbing, resting if you must, but not giving up midway. It all depends on your will and power – the willpower.

Keep negative people long meters away from you; their presence is a threat to your high self-esteem! Job, the man of God kept his wife afar before he could make it again!

--- Israelmore Ayivor, The Great Hand Book of Quotes ---

Your relationships are a great investment - probably the richest investment that you could ever have. Like any other shrewd investor, you don't want to keep dead investments. Investments that consume more than they bring are not worth keeping. Keep reviewing your relationships, and those like branches that no longer bear fruits, prune them off so that those that bear fruits can have healthier ones.

Negative people are like a very low ceiling that prevents you from standing up, leave alone jumping. They affect your self-esteem, self-confidence, self-worth, and self-actualization. They are a disaster to your wellbeing. The earlier you keep them off the better you are back on track to optimizing your potential to becoming all you've ever dreamt of becoming.

Life hurts when you are constrained. Frustrations are simply the energy of a potential that has not been allowed to actualize.

If you associate yourself with a change maker, Your life will, by all means, become better.
You will wink at challenges and begin to think.
In times of frustrations, you will not sink.

If you miss the way to a great destination, Just look for those going in that direction.

Mount the shoulders of a giant believer
And you will become a great achiever.

People around you determine your speed.
They will influence the growth of your seed.
People you are around will decide your strength
And also the figure of your success' length
I trust you want to become a better you.

It matters, what your associates plan to do.
It depends, where your companions want to go.
It relies on what your friends believe and know.
Quit friendships that build you nothing

Choose friends who bring out of you something
One iron sharpens another iron
Go along with great people and ride on."

-- Israelmore Ayivor, Become a Better You --

If you really want to change the way you have been, then, seek change-makers in your relationships. Yes, people who show you a different perspective of life; People who see opportunities in what you can only see as problems; people who are ready to take your hand and help you make a giant leap over an obstacle; people who are ready and willing to go an extra mile just to make sure that you don't give on your resolve. These are the change-makers that you need! Life will stop hurting when you embrace such people.

Tips to help you engender the right association;

1. Know **what** you want out of this association

2. Know **why** you need what you want in this association

3. Know **where** to get the people with what you need

4. Determine **when** to meet the people with what you need

5. Establish **how** to get the people with what you need

There are certain natures of which the mutual influence is such that, the more they say, the more they have to say. For these out of association grows adhesion, and out of adhesion, amalgamation.

--- Charlotte Brontë, Villette ---

Step Six: Give meaning to *your life*

The miracle is not to walk on water. The miracle is to walk on the green earth, dwelling deeply in the present moment and feeling truly alive.

*--- **Thich Nhat Hanh** ---*

Life is so simple, life is so basic. Yet, many of us waste it chasing glitters beyond the horizon. Do we have time just to walk barefoot on grass and just feel its effect beneath our feet? Do we have time just to watch the marvels of a waterfall and just be without thoughts ringing about our job, business, yesterday and tomorrow?

The greatest of miracles happen not in great things but in the small things that we overlook. Just watch safari ants matching and building their path, guarding and ferrying foodstuff to their about-to-be kingdom. As blind as they are, they probably work more miracles than that which we achieve in bellowing factories.

The real meaning of life is not in the big things but in the small things that we so often take for granted. Life hurts when we take for granted small things like just sitting calm and taking a deep breath; playing around just to have fun; tending to a small garden – be it in your backyard or in your in-house pot; spending time to fetch clean, natural, organic ingredients for the meal that you are going to cook; playing with your lovely pet; having time to play with children; visiting and spending time with your parents/grandparents, etc.

It is such small activities that absorb the shocks of the hurts of life leaving you to ride comfortably to your life's destiny.

"Many people die with their music still in them. Why is this so? Too often it is because they are always getting ready to live. Before they know it, time runs out."

--- Oliver Wendell Holmes ---

Have you ever postponed that nice stanza of poetry that just ran in the mind simply to be at a certain on time? Have you ever muted that sound of music that had started reverberating in your vocals simply because it wasn't the 'right' time? Well, those were the moments of true living that you wished away as you were getting ready to live them later, only for the 'right' time to come and you realize that the poem and the lyric are gone to the world of the forgotten never to come back. That's a piece of life that died with the poem and the music, forever!

Opportunities such as these are plenty and come spontaneously. They knock quite often. It all about how prepared you are to grab them and drink from the sweet potion they present. Life hurts when you miss partaking from such opportunities simply because you weren't prepared.

Carry with you a pen and a notebook. Carry with you a camera. Carry with you a voice recorder. These are the little things that you can carry around without feeling weighty yet can grab great moments. Yes, life hurts when you let opportunities fizzle away from you. Seize the moment!

"Eternal life belongs to those who live in the present"

--- Ludwig Wittgenstein ---

Just as we keep away our poems and music, it is the very same we keep away our eternal life. A life not fully lived in its very moment is a life that has lost its eternity. A poem lost is a poem untold. A piece of music lost is music unsung.

How else would we have impacted on others if not through that poem and music? How would have our loved ones been if they had listened to our poem and danced to our music? What a lasting inspiration would you have bequeathed your loved ones had they listened to your poem and danced to your music?

Eternal life is that life that continues to impact your loved ones and others for years and years, long after you are gone. Eternal life doesn't depend on how long you live but on how much you transformed yourself to impact positively on others such as to continue bequeathing a lasting legacy generation after generation.

Eternal life is a one lived fully in the moment of now. It is a one that bequeaths others a legacy that is free from hurts and salvages them from their very own hurts.

The fact that your coming into birth was an effort of many people and your very upbringing an effort of even a bigger multitude, it simply means you owe your life not just to you but many others - gone, living and yet to come. Live your life so that others may easily live.

Leave a path so that others may have their journeys easier because you lived to create it. This is the essence of eternity.

LIFE is a dichotomy of two sets of words;

1. Lasting inspiration
2. Forever energized – (see next step 7)

Lasting Inspiration

Lasting inspiration is that kind of inspiration that does not extinguish. That is, an inspiration that remains relevant generation after generation and its relevance seems not to have any predictable or foreseeable expiry date. It is a healing balm to others' life hurts.

To have a lasting inspiration to others so that they too may lead a healthy, happy and long life, you need to have a great lifestyle.

A great lifestyle – the best way to have a lasting inspiration

A great lifestyle is a lifestyle that enables you to have peace, joy, serenity and be in harmony with yourself, the nature of beings and the nature of things. In essence, it is a life that helps you to be free from hurts – frictions and conflicts with your nature of being and the nature of things. Such a lifestyle encompasses the following;

1. The right mindset – seek to change your mindset. Boost your willpower. Take control of your situation. Take charge of your emotions. Be focused. Enjoy your moment!

2. A healthy diet – have a clean, healthy, natural, balanced diet.

3. Physical fitness – keep off the sedentary lifestyle. Don't just engage yourself in

physical exercises alone. Don't just focus on the gym. Also, focus on doing manual work that can enhance your activity. Participate in active charity activities such as cooking for the destitute, the elderly and the needy. Participate in building shelters for the displaced, the disaster-stricken, the homeless, and others.

4. Wholesome wellbeing – practice self-compassion (see next step)

Step Seven: Practice Self Compassion

You can only love yourself as much as you love others. So, love others so that you can be able to love yourself.

Self-compassion is being considerate enough to understand your world flows from inside into the outer world. What gets out reflects that which is inside. Self-compassion is not selfishness or denying others of compassion but realizing that ultimately, like that vehicle that ferries others, it has to be well within its engine to make the journey safer, enjoyable and achievable. Thus, self-compassion is a kind of compassion turned inside out.

"I found in my research that the biggest reason people aren't more self-compassionate is that they are afraid they'll become self-indulgent. They believe self-criticism is what keeps them in line. Most people have gotten it wrong because our culture says being hard on yourself is the way to be"

--- Dr. Kirstin Neff ---

To practice, self-compassion is to be in love with your being. It is to know without self-love actualized through action to relieve yourself of your very own challenges and suffering, you cannot achieve the same of others. You have to begin from inside.

You have to tend to your own wound with tender love and understanding its sources and its eventual end. You have to heal your wounds. Only then, can you be able to do the same to others.

Having self-love accompanied by faith in your being is the true healing balm to your trauma when life hurts.

"The love that you give is the only love that you keep"

Love is the fuel that drives compassion. Without love, there cannot exist in compassion. To be compassionate is to express love in deeds. There is no way you can love others without first loving yourself. All else will be a pretense. Love radiates from inside to outside. Without it being inside, it can't be outside.

When it comes to love and compassion, you can only receive as much as you give. Thus, if you have to love yourself dearly, then, you have to love others dearly for it is in loving others that you are capable of loving yourself and not the other way round.

Thus, self-compassion must, for its very own survival, be externalized into compassion for others. This is where it derives its muscular strength and fitness.

"You live longer once you realize that any time spent being unhappy is wasted."

--- Ruth E. Renkl ---

Self-pity, anger, remorse, bitterness are all life hurts that are symptomatic of pain for that which happened in the past. They are signs of a lack of happiness. It is not that you cannot be happy with pain. But, pain must not degenerate into self-pity, anger, remorse, and bitterness.

You must own your pain. To own it is to accept that what happened is irreversible and it had its consequences which you are experiencing right now. You have to detach yourself from this sensitivity and experience pain for what it really is – a crying call for healing. Focus on healing.

Be nice yourself

"This is a moment of suffering.

Suffering is part of life.

May I be kind to myself at this moment.

May I give myself the compassion I need."

--- Kristin Neff ---

Life is tough sometimes. Acceptance of pain without reacting to it brings emotional intelligence. Treat yourself for 10 minutes a day with a soft word, a hand on heart, and a level of understanding that what you are going through is painful. You are human, and as a human, you will experience pain and suffering and if you try to avoid this emotional experience through avoidance behaviors such as drugs or alcohol you suffer further.

Forever Energized

Forever Energized simply means that this Lasting Inspiration does not extinguish. It is self-energizing, generations after generations. It is an inspiration that in itself contains a self-propelled life force. Whoever comes into its manifestation gets energized by its being.

Those legendary personalities that lived hundreds to thousands of years ago, we have never seen them in our lifetime. We never witnessed their deeds. But, from their histories, we are inspired by their words and deeds.

Whenever we read their history, we simply get inspired and energized as if we are actually getting words straight from their mouths and actually benefiting from their deeds.

This is simply because their words and deeds had a lasting inspiration. And these words and deeds are forever energized by those who read about them and draw from them the inherent power within them.

To be forever energized, you need to have a legacy worth bequeathing your family, your community, your generation and many other generations to come.

That legacy should not be a transmission of life hurts but a transmission of the joys and happiness of a life triumphant over life hurts.

Leaving a legacy worth bequeathing – The best way to be forever energized

A legacy worth bequeathing is a legacy that;

1. Impacted on people's lives while you lived
2. Will continue to impact people's for many years long after you have gone

Compassion: The best way to impact on people's lives while you live

Compassion can simply be stated as a passionate love for humanity. Compassion is a feeling that arises when you are confronted with the suffering of another that pushes you to have an inner compulsion, force or desire to relieve that suffering.

Studies have indicated that compassion is a necessity for the survival of the human species.

The benefits of compassion are many and immense. The following are just but a few of them;

- Compassion makes us feel good. Studies have found out that a compassionate deed triggers the 'feel good' part of our brain circuitry responsible for pleasure and reward thus leading happiness.

- Being compassionate boosts the positive effects of the Vagus nerve thus helping to slow down the heart rate which, in the long-run serves to reduce the risk of heart disease.

- Compassion lowers the stress hormones in the blood system and saliva thus boosting the immune system while helping people to become more resilient to stress.

- Compassion reduces worries about the past and anxiety about the future thus helping to prevent risks of mental disorder.

- Compassion triggers neurons in the brain which are responsible for parental nurturance thus helping to develop and boosts one's caregiving attributes which are important in personal development and leadership.

- Compassion boosts relationships by engendering optimism and supportive communication between partners.

- Compassion helps to build strong bonds for lasting friendships. Studies have shown that when people set a goal to support one another compassionately, they experienced increased satisfaction and growth in their common endeavors.

- Compassion helps to mold us into characters that are less vindictive, less jealous and less selfish.

- Compassion helps us strengthen our moral principles and that contributes to building a cohesive team, group, or society.

- Compassion at work has been proven to boost productivity, lower employee turnover and maximize reward to all stakeholders.

- Studies have proven that more compassionate societies have less destitute, fewer crime rates and generally, more happiness.

- Compassion makes people more socially adept, less vulnerable to loneliness, anger, and depression. These, in turn, reduce the stress that causes harm to the immune systems leading to healthier, longer and happier lives.

The following are some of the tips that can help you build and boost your compassion;

- See the good in others – everyone has a positive side in life. Focusing overly on the negative negates our spirit of compassion.

- Focus on commonalities rather than differences – we are all different. This is the essence of diversity. However, focusing on what differentiates us from that which unites us will rob our sense of compassion.

- Calm your inner worries. You cannot be compassionate if you are overwhelmed by inner worries, anxiety, and regrets. The best way to calm your inner worries is through mindfulness and meditation.

- Encourage cooperation rather than competition – competition draws the animal instinct in us that seeks override or even trample on others in order to achieve success. This denies us the desire for compassion. When we cooperate to see the importance of others in our joint endeavor and the desire to help them for all of us to succeed.

- See people as beings rather than objects – when you focus so much on the product rather than the people producing it, you end seeing people as objects of production rather than human beings who have senses, feelings, and emotions. This makes you less compassionate.

- Avoid playing the blame game – not all of us are fortunate. Some are less fortunate. Blaming people for their misfortunes rather than seeking to help them overcome them or relieve their harsh effects robs us of our compassion.

- Help to prevent inequality – inequality is bred by some feeling a sense of entitlement to a higher status than the rest.

- Learn to appreciate and enjoy your moments of compassion – the best way to reinforce your compassion is to see the good you've done to others and appreciate the benefit they have received rather than how they have responded to your compassion. This way, you wouldn't regret it when some become thankless.

- In acts of compassion, avoid absorbing the problem – it is easy to get so much absorbed into acts of compassion such that we absorb the problem. Help others as much as you can but not more than you can as this can drain off your energy, lead to fatigue and more problems to your health thus cutting down on your compassion lifespan.

- Cultivate compassion in others – teach your children, your family, your friends and your community about compassion. This is the best way to spread the goodness and also the best way to lower the burden that you shoulder in exercising compassion.

How to impact people's lives for many years long after you are gone

Eternally impacting on people is never such an easy adventure. It involves quite a lot. The following are some steps involved in impacting on people's lives for many years long after you are gone;

1. **Explore people** – in exploring people, you make an active conscious undertaking to know people. This conscious undertaking involves exploring people's culture, lifestyle, mindset, habits, attitudes and the like.

2. **Learn people** – in learning people, you evaluation the outcome of your

exploration and do an analysis of this outcome and draw out conclusions.

3. **Understand people** – to understand people is to comprehend the lessons drawn from learning them.

4. **Accept people** – in accepting people, you take people the way they are based on your understanding of them without apportioning judgment, opinions, biases, and prejudices.

5. **Appreciate people** – to appreciate people is to accept them and know that in them there is a higher good in their humanness.

6. **Educate people** – understanding, accepting and appreciating people is not about surrendering to their state of being. It is arriving at the greater good in them. Once you arrive at the greater good in them, you seek, through education, to advance this greater good so that greater benefit can be derived from them for the better of humanity. There is a Chinese

proverb that goes: if you want to plan for a season, plant rice; if you want to plan for a decade, plant tree; if you plan for a lifetime, educate people.

7. **Uplift people** – once you educate people, they become enlightened. They come to that self-awareness and awareness of the environment and their role in their being, the nature of beings and the nature of things. To uplift them is to empower them with the necessary resources so that that they can attain a higher level of the greater good.

8. **Inspire people** – once people are uplifted, they need to be self-propelled in order to continue climbing the staircase of greatness. They need to draw that inner energy inherent in them to achieve this. Lack of motivation or willpower can prevent them from achieving this. To inspire people is to ignite this willpower in them to draw upon this inherent

energy into propelling themselves to higher pedestals of the greater good.

CONCLUSION

Thank you for acquiring this book and reading it through to this end.

This book, **Being an Empath:** *A Complete Survival Guide to Understand Empaths and Develop Empathy Abilities, Improve Your Emotional Intelligence, and Learn Strategies to Protect Yourself from Energy Vampires*, is purposely written to clear misunderstandings about empaths and enable them to avoid succumbing to conformity that maims their nature and mutes their voice.

I hope you have learned **how to discover yourself, improve your wellbeing and get the best out of your nature.** It is also my sincere hope that you have been inspired enough to share information provided in this book by encouraging fellow empaths, your loved ones, friends and others to get a copy of this book so that they too can gain this in-depth understanding of the nature of empaths.

Again, thank you for acquiring this book.

Good Luck!

Made in the USA
Columbia, SC
23 December 2021

52676283R10211